Freed by Grace

Freed by Grace

Release from
Life's Imprisonments

Hal Brady

DIMENSIONS
FOR LIVING
NASHVILLE

FREED BY GRACE: RELEASE FROM LIFE'S IMPRISONMENTS

Copyright © 1998 by Dimensions for Living

This book is printed on acid-free paper.

Cataloguing-in-Publication Data is available from the Library of Congress.

Most Scripture quotations are from the New Revised Standard Version of the Bible. Copyright 1989 by the Division of Christian Education of the National Council of the Churches of Christ in the USA. Used by permission.

Those noted RSV are from the Revised Standard Version of the Bible, copyright 1946, 1952, 1971 by the Division of Christian Education of the National Council of the Churches of Christ in the USA. Used by permission.

Those noted KJV are from the King James Version Bible.

That noted NEB is from *The New English Bible.* © The Delegates of the Oxford University Press and The Syndics of the Cambridge University Press 1961, 1970. Reprinted by permission.

98 99 00 01 02 03 04 05 06 07 — 10 9 8 7 6 5 4 3 2 1

MANUFACTURED IN THE UNITED STATES OF AMERICA

To Myron,
in love and appreciation
for her faithful support
in sharing my journey

Contents

Introduction

Serving Time

Not long ago, I stood up with a young friend as he faced the judge in a crowded court room. My young friend was there for driving an automobile while under the influence of alcohol. As his pastor, I wanted to be there with and for him and his family. Since this remorseful young man had been stopped on a previous occasion for a similar offense, I was concerned about the judge's verdict.

Though it was obvious the young man had acknowledged his mistake, the judge, under the confines of the law, had set more stringent standards for a second offense. Consequently, my friend received a substantial fine, temporary revocation of his driver's license, and forty-eight hours in detention in the county jail. As I watched the young man walk down the hall in the custody of a law officer to serve his time in jail, I could not help but think of the countless imprisonments life holds for each one of us.

By now, my young friend has served his time, has prayerfully learned a lesson, and is enjoying the freedom of release. But so many of us are still "serving time." Individuals are held captive by all sorts of devastating confinements, faulty emotions, and cruel addictions. In reality, none of us has escaped this commonality of our existence.

At times we are all victims of grumbling, inferiority, loneliness, worry, depression, grief, discouragement, fear, stress, anger, giving up, and success. These twelve "prisons" are more than simply my own approach to facing imprisonments; they are also this prisoner's attempt to share with others the joyful hope that promises release. Fortunately, we aren't compelled to serve out a life sentence in these prisons: God's grace sets us free! Faith and Scripture show the way out, and they also help us to recognize the nature of our troubles and what we can do, through God, to change the way we see ourselves and handle our circumstances.

A few years ago, I was confined to a hospital room for several weeks with infectious hepatitis. No visitors were allowed. Peeping out into the hall one day, I discovered a note attached to my door. A minister friend had left his card with these words: "God's grace is sufficient." It *was,* and it *is!* Let God give you the key to unlock your prison doors.

"Everybody Does It" Doesn't Help

Therefore, my beloved, just as you have always obeyed me, not only in my presence, but much more now in my absence, work out your own salvation with fear and trembling; for it is God who is at work in you, enabling you both to will and to work for his good pleasure.

Do all things without murmuring and arguing, so that you may be blameless and innocent, children of God without blemish in the midst of a crooked and perverse generation, in which you shine like stars in the world. It is by your holding fast to the word of life that I can boast on the day of Christ that I did not run in vain or labor in vain. But even if I am being poured out as a libation over the sacrifice and the offering of your faith, I am glad and rejoice with all of you—and in the same way you also must be glad and rejoice with me.

Philippians 2:12-18

A woman in her eighties, rigid and conservative, had become cynical. She thought everything modern was bad and every new change was a disaster. She complained to her pastor, "Pastor, it's a good time to be dead!"

Now few of us would be pleased at being compared with this glum person. But *most* of us, if we are honest, do not have much room to brag. We know that one of the things we do best—and perhaps most frequently—is grumble. And our grumbling tends to spill over into everything else. God may have delivered us from sin's bondage, all right, but we still find plenty of things that we don't like.

Let's face it—we are a bunch of grumblers. I'm talking about people who never rise above negativism. These people always want to complain. Nothing is ever right, and they are never content. At church, "that's not the way we used to do it." At school, "the teacher's not fair to my child." At work, "the boss is unreasonable" or "the employee wastes time." At home, "teenagers are in a different orbit" or "the spouse just doesn't understand." With the government, "my taxes are too high." If the truth be told, maybe there are few who grumble *all* the time. Most of us are really *"recovering* grumblers." But it is so easy to fall back into old habits.

An anonymous poet described the members of "The Grumble Family" this way:

There's a family nobody likes to meet,
They live, it is said, on Complaining Street,
In the city of Never-are-Satisfied,
The river of Discontent beside.
They growl at that and they growl at this,
Whatever comes there is something amiss;
And whether their situation be high or humble,
They are known by the name of Grumble.

The weather is always too hot or cold,
Summer and winter alike they scold;
Nothing goes right with the folks you meet
Down on that gloomy Complaining Street.
They growl at the rain and they growl at the sun,
In fact, their growling is never done.
And if everything pleased them, there isn't a doubt
They'd growl that they'd nothing to grumble about.
. . . .
So it is wisest to keep our feet
From wandering into Complaining Street;
And never to growl, whatever we do,
Lest we be mistaken for Grumblers, too.
Let us learn to walk with a smile and song,

No matter if things do sometimes go wrong,
And then, be our station high or humble,
We'll never belong to the family of Grumble!

In the apostle Paul's letter to the Philippians, he challenges people who have received God's grace to live up to their calling. Paul says, "Only, live your life in a manner worthy of the gospel of Christ" (1:27), and, "Do all things without grumbling" (2:14, RSV). Paul is saying that one of the marks of the abundant life or salvation is not only unity and harmony, but wholeness. "Do all things without grumbling," he says. Grumbling takes away from our wholeness. It reduces us in our relationships—with God, with one another, and with ourselves.

Grumbling Is Not Very Flattering

One old story tells of a hound dog sitting in a country store, howling his head off. A stranger came in and said to the storekeeper, "What's the matter with that dog?"

The storekeeper said, "He's sitting on a cocklebur."

"Then," asked the stranger, "why doesn't he get off?"

"Because," replied the storekeeper, "he'd rather holler!"

So often, that's true of *us,* isn't it? We'd rather grumble. Like the Israelites of old, we forget the graciousness of God in our lives. There is some indication that when Paul was urging the "grumble-free" life, he was thinking of the grumbling and disobedience of the children of Israel in the wilderness under Moses. In the Exodus narrative, these grumblings of Israel are mentioned no less than four times.

The Israelites were camping at Rephidim. They wanted water, and they wanted it pronto. They didn't *ask* Moses for it; they *demanded* it of him. They grumbled, "Give us water to drink! Why did you bring us out of Egypt to die in the wilderness?" (Exodus 17:2-3, paraphrased).

How quickly the Israelites had forgotten the continuing graciousness of God in their lives! Never mind the fact that God in God's grace had already provided them a way out of Egypt. Never mind that God had delivered them from an angry, pursuing Pharaoh. Never mind that God had already provided them with their daily manna. Never mind that God had chosen them as God's people. They wanted water, and they wanted it now. In desperation, Moses turned to God: "O God, what shall I do? These people are ready to kill me" (Exodus 17:4, paraphrased). But God in God's grace heard Moses with tender mercy and enormous patience, and responded with the water.

The psalmist said, "Bless the Lord, O my soul, / and all that is within me, / bless his holy name. / Bless the Lord, O my soul, / and do not forget all his benefits" (Psalm 103:1-2). Grumbling is an indication that we have forgotten the continuing graciousness of God in our lives.

And how quickly we forget! For example, we frequently grumble about the problem of growing older. As someone expressed it:

You know you are getting older when you try to straighten out the wrinkles in your socks, only to find out you aren't wearing any.

You know you are getting older when you stop patting yourself on the back and start patting yourself under the chin.

You know you are getting older when you feel like the night before, and you haven't been anywhere.

You know you are getting older when a fortune teller offers to read your face.

You know you are getting older when you sink your teeth into a steak and they stay there.

We forget that 150 years ago, approximately 2.5 percent of North American citizens were over the age of sixty-five. Today, that number has grown to more than 10 percent. In other words, if we were living in 1850, many of today's persons over sixty-five wouldn't have these "problems," because they'd already be dead!

Robert Fulghum, the noted author, said that visiting his own grave "has the reliable capacity to untwist the snarls in my mind and soul." Putting it another way, visiting his grave helps him gain a perspective on his grumbling. Fulghum said, "On one visit, I realized that if I had died that day, and if my wife were to put an honest epitaph on my headstone, it would say, 'Here lies a jackass—too [griped] off to live long." Then he said, "How I'd hate to die mad." [1] Visiting his own grave had helped Fulghum recognize the blessing of his wife. And it helped to illustrate for him what may not be obvious enough to most of us in our own lives: Grumbling is not very flattering.

Grumbling Is a Sign of the B.C.

A man had just completed his transaction at the bank. The teller said to him, "Have a nice day." To which, the man growled his reply, "I've already made alternative plans." In our own personal experience, this type of response is a sign of the B.C.—our life "before Christ." Or, at least, it's a sign of our initial beginnings in our life with Christ.

Paul says, "Work out your own salvation . . . ; for it is God who is at work in you, enabling you both to will and to work for his good pleasure" (Philippians 2:12b-13). The Greek word Paul uses for "work out"—*katergazomai*—has the idea of completion. It is as if Paul said, "Don't stop half way; don't be satisfied with a partial salvation. Keep on working it out until the work of salvation is fully and finally formed in you."

In my mind, I see Emmett Smith of the Dallas Cowboys, running down the field toward the goal line, the ball tucked away under his arm. He's got a clear field ahead, the game is on the line, and there are only a few seconds left to play. There isn't another player within twenty yards of Emmett. The radio announcer reports, with mounting excitement, "He's at the fifty, the forty-five, the forty, the thirty-five . . ." And then, the announcer exclaims in astonishment, "Folks, you are not going to *believe* it! Emmett Smith has just walked off the field at the thirty-five-yard line and has taken a seat on the bench! The Cowboys lose!"

Translate that into Paul's concern for our salvation: "Don't stop half way. Don't be satisfied with a partial salvation. Keep on working it out until the work of salvation is fully and finally formed in you." John Wesley admonished his young preachers to "groan after perfection," to struggle to be better, to keep the door open so that God could continue the perfection process.

Grumbling is a sign of the B.C., a sign of incompleteness. It is a mark of arrested spiritual development, a sign of not growing in grace. And it is characteristic of a life chained to self-interest.

Some time ago in a singles Bible study I led, we were talking about Paul's admonition to the Colossians and to us. He gives a reminder that we died in Christ, we are raised with Christ, we live in Christ, we are hidden in Christ, and we are going to be glorified with Christ. Then Paul says, in view of our wonderful relationship with Christ, we have a great responsibility, and that is to "seek the things that are above" (Colossians 3:1). This means putting off the old nature, which includes grumbling, and putting on the new, which means having compassion, kindness, lowliness, meekness, patience, forgiveness, and so on.

A woman once came to writer Ralph Waldo Emerson and said that the world was coming to an end. Emerson replied, "That's all right, I can get along without it." And so can we—*especially* if it's the world of our old nature.

Grumbling Becomes Graciousness Through Christ

Author Philip Yancey asked, "*Why am I a Christian?*" He then said that he had reduced his answers to two: "(1) the lack of good alternatives, and (2) Jesus. . . . Jesus stands up to scrutiny. He is who I want my God to be." [2]

Only having the mind of Christ can free us from our negativism. It's the real test of a Christian—not creeds, sacraments, rites, or correct morals. It's a disposition of mind. Paul says to the Philippians, "Let the same mind be in you that was in Christ Jesus" (Philippians 2:5). How do we let the mind of Christ be our mind?

Paul says, "Work out your own salvation . . . for God is at work in you." So we work out our salvation not by *might*; we can't do it all by ourselves. Not by *magic;* we can't do it through superstitions. But we *can* work out our salvation by *the mercy of God.* God got us where we are today. God has started us on our way. And God will never quit what God starts. Having the mind of Christ is a gift that we receive, respond to, and follow.

A friend of mine had his first golf lesson. After the lesson, he asked the golf pro instructor, "What is the basic thing I need?" The instructor replied, "A miracle!" That's really what all of us need. And God has given us the miracle in Christ.

Not long ago, I was riding in the car with an acquaintance. In the middle of our conversation about some other matter, he suddenly turned to me and said, "Hal, I just wasn't *happy* until I met him." "Him *who*?" I asked. "Jesus," he replied.

Like this man, many of us just aren't *happy,* and we may not even be able to tell you why. As individuals and as a society, we grumble and complain so much that it brings us down, along with everybody else around us. Grumbling is one of the most insidious imprisonments of all—most of us don't even recognize it as a problem, and therefore we never realize the residual damage of its negative effects in our lives. God wants something better than this for us—for *each one of us.*

By having the mind of Christ—being open to God's working through us—we begin to change our very nature, letting graciousness kick in, and throwing grumbling out with the trash.

Getting in Touch with the Real You

When the Pharisees heard that he had silenced the Sadducees, they gathered together, and one of them, a lawyer, asked him a question to test him. "Teacher, which commandment in the law is the greatest?" He said to him, " 'You shall love the Lord your God with all your heart, and with all your soul, and with all your mind.' This is the greatest and first commandment. And a second is like it: 'You shall love your neighbor as yourself.' On these two commandments hang all the law and the prophets."

Matthew 22:34-40

Reuel Howe, renowned pastoral counselor and educator, tells of a seminar participant named Joe. Joe sat in a seminar for five straight days and offered absolutely nothing to the conversation—he never said a word. "Again and again efforts were made to draw him in because he looked lonely and miserable. Finally, he said, 'I haven't spoken because I don't feel that I have anything worth saying. I'd rather listen.' In the exchange that followed he admitted that he was tired of listening and that he would like to contribute. He added that he felt inferior because of what he regarded as an inadequate education." [1]

Like Joe, many people in our world today are jailed by a low sense of self-esteem. The cause may be different, but the condition is the same. For the most part, these people feel inadequate and worthless. Many are depressed.

A tall, good-looking young man came to a minister's study one day to talk. The young man obviously had a lot to live for, but he had a troubled outlook. He had just taken a series of tests for admission to college, and the results had not been encouraging. "They tell me," he said, "I just can't cut it." [2]

That young man was probably speaking for a number of us. Sometimes we feel that we just can't cut it. We simply do not have a high enough opinion of ourselves. And unfortunately, this attitude causes us to run and hide, even from ourselves. It keeps us from loving God and others, and it torpedoes our living life at its best.

Specifically, low self-esteem hurts our relationships. It keeps us isolated from one another. When our major concern is with our own inferiority or inadequacy, we live to ourselves. We are afraid to venture out into relationships—afraid of rejection, afraid of failure, afraid of comparison.

I remember in high school the great difficulty I had talking on the telephone to a girl I liked. I would make the call and then struggle for the words. "Hello," she would answer. I would reply, "This is Hal—Hal Brady." I would always hate having to say that: "This is Hal—Hal Brady" . . . and then tongue-tied silence. Not exactly the best way to start a relationship.

Remember the parable of the talents? A man preparing to take a long trip gathered his servants. The man had a great deal of money, and he distributed it to his servants to care for while he was away. To one servant he gave five talents (large units of money), to another he gave two, and to another he gave one. When the master returned after a long absence, he found that the servants to whom he had given five and two talents each had wisely invested the money and were able to give back to the master twice as much as he had given them. But the servant who had been given one talent had not invested his money, and instead had buried his talent in the ground; since the talent had earned no interest, the servant was only able to give back to the master the original amount. The servant was condemned by his master for being so lazy (Matthew 25:14-30).

Why had this one-talent servant buried his talent in the ground? Because he was afraid—afraid of his master's judgment, afraid of being compared to the five-talent and two-talent servants, afraid of risking. So, feeling inadequate and inferior, the one-talent servant did nothing. This is one of the tragic dangers of inferiority: the waste of human possibility.

The Scripture passage in Matthew 22 addresses this sense of inferiority, inadequacy, and worthlessness. In answer to the lawyer's question about the Great Commandment, Jesus said, " 'You shall love the Lord your God with all your heart, and with all your soul, and with all your mind.' This is the greatest and first commandment. And a second is like it: 'You shall love your neighbor as yourself' " (verses 37-39). When we first read these verses, we are so focused on the ideas of loving God and loving neighbor that we almost overlook the key component to the entire process—the words *as yourself.* Paint these words boldly across the horizon of your mind and heart. "As yourself." It all begins here, with you, with each one of us as individuals. If we are truly to love God and our neighbors, we must first love ourselves.

So how do we come to love ourselves and overcome our feelings of inferiority, inadequacy, and worthlessness? Well, it won't happen overnight; but it *can* happen.

We Can Love Ourselves by Remembering
That It Is God's Assessment of Us That Counts

John B. Rogers Jr., in his book *In Him Is Life,* writes that "among the anecdotes concerning the legendary Benjamin Jowett of Baloil College, Oxford, is that once at a faculty reception, an effusive young woman said to him, 'Oh, doctor, you believe in God; do tell me about it!' The great teacher smiled and replied, 'That, my dear lady, is a very unimportant question. What is more significant is that God believes in me.' " [3]

How do we begin to love ourselves? We start with God. We start with God's believing in us. We start with God's assessment of us. Each one of us is a child of God, and there is nothing inferior or second-best about that.

Too many of us, however, measure our worth not by God, but by some distorted reflection from our past or present. Like other personality traits, our self-image has its roots in our early life. If we are given positive feedback from parents, friends, colleagues, and others, then more than likely we will develop a positive self-evaluation. On the other hand, if these same people in our lives *don't* give us this type of positive reinforcement, we will develop a negative self-evaluation. We will develop feelings of inferiority, inadequacy, and worthlessness. One particular poem shows this clearly. A young boy is brimming with excitement as he proudly tells his father that he got two A's on his report card. When his father asks him why didn't he get three, the boy's spirit is instantly crushed and his self-worth drained. But in the house just down the street, another boy gleefully reports two A's on *his* card, and his father, beaming with pride, says, "I'm glad you belong to me." [4] The same situation was played out in two different locations, with two very different outcomes. And more likely than not, the lad who got the praise and encouragement will be the one to succeed, to excel, to flourish.

More important than what *others* think of us is what *God* thinks of us. Author Wilson O. Weldon illustrates this well:

One day, an elderly man in a Southern town was talking: "I don't amount to much in this town," he said. "I have not been what [people] call 'successful.' But I think I do amount to something with God. I can forget what people around here think of me when I remember what God thinks of me." [5]

Who are we to feel inferior when God loves us so intentionally? Nothing says it better than John 3:16: "For God so loved the world that he gave his only Son, so that everyone who believes in him may not perish but may have eternal life."

Who are we to feel inferior when God created us in God's own image? No other part of God's creation is made in God's image. We are literally God's masterpieces, God's greatest works! So why do we stand in awe of the beauty of the mountains, the vastness of the sea, the mystery of space, the reality of a flower . . . and at the same time, disparage ourselves? Are we not of more value than all of these?

Who are we to feel inferior when Jesus Christ died for us?

Who are we to feel inferior when God made us for eternity?

And who are we to feel inferior when the Holy Spirit resides in us? This is the same Holy Spirit of which the writer of John's epistle says, "For the one who is in you is greater than the one who is in the world" (1 John 4:4). Where do we get our idea of our self-worth? Do we get it from some distorted reflection of our past or present? Or do we get it from God? To paraphrase Weldon's elderly gentleman in the Southern town, "We can forget what people around here think of us when we remember what *God* thinks of us."

We Can Love Ourselves by Getting Our Heads on Straight

Some think that while it is right to love other people, it is sinful to love ourselves. But as Dr. James Mallory, a Christian psychiatrist, observed:

A person who has truly experinced this powerful love of God and who realizes how much he is loved of God is also better able to love himself. As many have recognized, without a healthy love for ourselves, we are unable to love others. As we properly love ourselves, we are less bound by self-consciousness and do not need to spend so much emotional energy trying to repair our sense of worth. We are able to see others as persons rather than as objects we may use to patch up our egos.[6]

A young person was being interviewed by a theater owner for a job as an usher. "What would you do in case of fire?" he asked. "Oh, don't worry about me," the young man answered. "I'd get out all right." In those circumstances, that is not self-love, but rather a contemptible kind of selfishness. Selfishness is inevitably hurtful and destructive. Genuine self-love, on the other hand, is redemptive, healing, supporting, and ennobling.

Jesus verified the importance of self-love when he said, " 'You shall love the Lord your God with all your heart, and with all your soul, and with all your mind.' This is the greatest and first commandment. And a second is like it: 'You shall love your neighbor as yourself.' " *As Yourself!* In reality, we do not have two commandments here, but three: to love God, to love others, and to love yourself. But as far as Jesus is concerned, to love yourself should be the *second* commandment, for Jesus knew that it is only when we truly love ourselves that we can then properly love others. Simply put, *we can only transfer to others the attitude we have toward ourselves.*

David Seamands, past professor of pastoral ministries at Asbury Theological Seminary, said that after a revival meeting where he preached on proper self-love, a woman approached him. She said that she had attended church all her life, but that he was the first preacher "she had ever heard say that she was supposed to love herself. 'All this time, I thought that God wanted me to dislike myself in order to stay humble.' " [7]

This woman was beginning to get her head on straight. What about the rest of us?

We Can Love Ourselves by Reclaiming Our Uniqueness

I read somewhere that a Rembrandt painting had sold for over one million dollars. What makes some paint on a canvas worth so much, anyway? Well, to begin with, this was obviously a unique painting. Of all the millions of paintings painted since the beginning of time, there was no other in the world exactly like it. It was a rare Rembrandt original. Too, Rembrandt was a genius. He had a rare talent, and it was his talent that was being recognized.

And then there's you and me. Of all the billions of people that have lived on this planet throughout history, you and I are both one of a kind. There never has been and there never will be another person exactly like you or like me! Like a Rembrandt painting, each of us is an original. Each of us is special and unique.

There's an old story about a sixth-grade teacher who asked this question of her class: "What is there in the world today that was not here fifteen years ago?" She expected students to tell of some new invention or discovery.

One boy raised his hand, and the teacher asked him, "All right, Johnny, what is your answer?"

He replied, simply, "Me."

That little boy was wonderfully correct. Because I am unique, I do not have to be number one to make a contribution. Because I am unique, I can rise above all my low moods. Because I am unique, I am somebody.

I like the story of the lady who met a little boy and asked him his name. The boy replied, "My name is George Washington."

"I hope that you grow up to be like George Washington," the lady said.

The boy responded, "I cannot help being like George Washington, because that is who I am."

Be somebody! By God's grace, you *are* somebody.

Love God and love your neighbor *as you love yourself.*

When You're Lonely

His disciples said, "Yes, now you are speaking plainly, not in any figure of speech! Now we know that you know all things, and do not need to have anyone question you; by this we believe that you came from God." Jesus answered them, "Do you now believe? The hour is coming, indeed it has come, when you will be scattered, each one to his home, and you will leave me alone. Yet I am not alone because the Father is with me. I have said this to you, so that in me you may have peace. In the world you face persecution. But take courage; I have conquered the world!"

John 16:29-33

"When the unclean spirit has gone out of a person, it wanders through waterless regions looking for a resting place, but it finds none. Then it says, 'I will return to my house from which I came.' When it comes, it finds it empty, swept, and put in order. Then it goes and brings along seven other spirits more evil than itself, and they enter and live there; and the last state of that person is worse than the first. So will it be also with this evil generation."

Matthew 12:43-45

A television viewer sent me a complimentary letter following my sermon on the good Samaritan. She wrote: "Why did the sermon mean so much? Because I know what it means to be alone. I have been a widow for thirty-four years. I had no children (much to my sorrow), and I have no relatives close by. I'm eighty-four, somewhat housebound, and how well I know the loneliness of many who are 'passed by' daily."

That person's situation is all too common. One woman, divorced and mother of a four-year-old daughter, revealed: "You don't know how many times I go to bed at night and cry myself to sleep because I am alone."

After a civic club meeting, a middle-aged woman came forward with several of her friends. In the course of conversation, she said, "You will never know how lonely I am." Immediately the others nodded in agreement, and one of them said, "I guess that goes for all of us."

And, in reality, I guess it does. Whether you're a child in your first days of school, a teenager struggling to grow up, a college student in a new environment, a husband or wife away from home, a single person dealing with the issues of being single, a believer seeking to live ethically, a newcomer, an ill person, an older person, a minister, an executive, a widow or widower; at times, all of us are held captive by loneliness—the feeling of being disconnected or separated.

One caring physician who is concerned about his patients as whole persons says he has discovered that "ninety-nine out of a hundred individuals are lonely. The one who says he isn't probably is." [1] Loneliness is indeed a universal problem, and yet it imprisons each of us as *individuals*. Surprisingly, there is something positive to say about loneliness: It can cause us to look deeper into the resources of the Spirit, to become more aware of the needs of others, and to reexamine our own lifestyles. When and if that happens, then loneliness can be considered helpful. However, nothing can be quite positive enough about loneliness. Its pain is all too real.

Jesus knew loneliness. He came to his own people and was rejected by them. It made no difference to them that he was a local resident, one of their own. In addition, Jesus was denied and forsaken by his close, personal friends. Could there be any greater hurt? Jesus *must* have felt the agony and the lonely disappointment. And then there was Jesus' suffering on the cross; this is the most devastating loneliness of all. We hear him cry out, "My God, my God, why have you forsaken me?" (Matthew 27:46).

In John 16, there is yet another lonely event for Jesus. Here the disciples assure Jesus of their belief in and devotion to him. But Jesus does not believe them. He replies, "You will leave me alone. Yet I am not alone because the Father is with me" (verse 32*b*). In these precious words of Jesus, we find meaningful direction for coping with our loneliness.

In Jesus' parable in Matthew 12:43-45, we find a man possessed by an unclean spirit. With strong resolution, this man sweeps his mind clear, only to later suffer the return of the spirit and the invasion of "seven other spirits" more loathsome than the first. This parable shows us that we can't just sweep our lives clear of loneliness unless we fill the vacuum that is left with other things. In other words, to successfully cope, we must replace our loneliness with something else—something better.

We Can Replace Our Loneliness with an Active Mind

We may not always be able to change the situation we face, but we can do something about our response to that situation. Some of our loneliness is related to circumstances beyond our control. But often, we can do something about the life we live in our minds. God did not intend for us to be victims of self-pity, inner emptiness, or boredom.

Essentially, loneliness forces us to face ourselves. If we are prepared to listen for its message, loneliness tells us that in some respects, we have to take responsibility for our own lives. There are simply some things that no one else is going to do for us, that no one else *can* do for us. It is so easy to withdraw into ourselves. But while that withdrawal is sometimes useful and necessary, if we continually shut out the people, ideas, and events around us, we will soon find ourselves in deep trouble.

One of God's greatest gifts to us is the power to use our minds, the ability to think. And recognizing this can go a long way toward helping us deal with our loneliness. The poet Edward Dyer sensed the significance of this when he wrote:

My mind to me a kingdom is . . .
It excels all other bliss. . . .[2]

An active mind is an endless resource, as many who have been prisoners of war have discovered. A Hungarian physician who spent three years in Siberia as a prisoner of the Soviets humbly remarked that two things saved him: his faith in God and the resources of his mind. "Through the years," he said, "I had committed the Scriptures to memory, and poetry was my hobby."

Another illustration of the power of the disciplined mind to cope with loneliness is the imprisonment of Nelson Mandela. In one of his first post-release interviews, Mandela said that in his twenty-seven years of prison life, he "never felt despair." What an astounding statement for him to make: In twenty-seven years of imprisonment, he never felt despair! Mandela went on to explain that while in prison, he continually read novels and biographies, and in later years he was allowed to see films. Of the films he saw, Mandela said, "I did not concentrate on commercial pictures. I was more interested to see educational pictures." This remarkable man had turned his captivity into an opportunity to learn, to grow, to enrich himself in some way. This is the power and result of a disciplined mind.

The apostle Paul gave the Philippians some helpful advice about combating loneliness. In his letters to them, Paul said, "Finally, beloved, whatever is true, whatever is honorable, whatever is just, whatever is pure, whatever is pleasing, whatever is commendable, if there is any excellence and if there is anything worthy of praise, think about these things" (Philippians 4:8).

Just prior to writing these words, Paul expressed a strong hope: "Rejoice in the Lord always; again I will say, Rejoice" (Philippians 4:4). Joy, radiant joy, belongs to the person who disciplines his or her mind to think thoughts that are true, honest, just, pure, good, pleasing, and lovely.

At various times I have had the privilege of giving the address at a graduation commencement. As I have watched students walk across the platform to receive their diplomas, sadly I have known that for some, *this was it*. For some, this occasion was not a commencement—a beginning—but rather an ending. At this point, they would stop cultivating their minds and would grow no further. Gradually, they would become empty, lonely people.

It doesn't have to be this way. God has given us the power to do something about it. We can replace our loneliness with an active, disciplined mind.

We Can Replace Our Loneliness with a Noble Purpose

A person focused on some significant and noble purpose, some reason for being, may know brief moments of loneliness—but not for long!

The Old Testament's Nehemiah is a good example of how a noble purpose can replace one's loneliness. Nehemiah was in charge of rebuilding the walls of Jerusalem. It seemed such a hopeless, lonely task: The walls were in ruins, the people were scattered and deeply discouraged, and all around were the Arab enemies, doing everything in their power to stop Nehemiah. They ridiculed him and plotted against him, but Nehemiah toiled on at his lonely task. He said, "I am doing a great work and I cannot come down" (Nehemiah 6:3).

Such is the power of a significant purpose. Nehemiah was so engaged in his task of rebuilding the walls of Jerusalem that no obstacle—not even the terrible feeling of loneliness—could stop him.

Friederich Nietzsche once said that having a "why" to live for enables one to endure any kind of "how." The devastating loneliness that grinds most of us down can lead to a life that plays out with no useful purpose.

When you ask, "What am I supposed to do with my life?" the answer is always, "Something useful." We can begin to accomplish this by having a noble purpose.

We Can Replace Our Loneliness with a Willing Involvement

We nourish our loneliness and feed it when we focus our thoughts upon ourselves. Most of the lonely people I have personally known have lived primarily to themselves and *for* themselves.

On the other hand, loneliness can also be made worse by furious activity—rushing around until we are completely exhausted. Someone astutely observed that our flight from loneliness has plunged us into a frantic togetherness. We have clubs and organizations for every imaginable purpose—and some with no purpose at all—where people in great numbers come together and associate. But we only begin to overcome our loneliness as we genuinely enter into the lives and experiences of other people, including those who are lonely.

Someone once asked Dr. Karl Menninger, "Suppose you suspect that you're heading for a nervous breakdown. What should you do?" You'd think this great psychiatrist would suggest that you see a psychiatrist. But this is what he said: "Go straight to your front door, turn the knob, cross the street, and find somebody who needs you." As a pastor, I have experienced periods of loneliness. However, those times have not persisted for long because of my continual involvement in the needs of my parishioners. While trying to minister to others in their times and places of great need—such as hospitals and nursing homes, to name a few—I have found that my own loneliness dissipates. Getting involved is often a good way to help you forget your own woes and cares. Sometimes we can best help ourselves by working toward helping others.

We Can Replace Our Loneliness with Church Fellowship

At the risk of oversimplifying, I believe that there are three major problems in the world. I have come to this conclusion from my reading, counseling, and studying over the past thirty years. The three major problems are loneliness, meaninglessness, and indifference. And I believe Jesus Christ and the church are the solutions to all of those problems.

One specific solution for the problem of loneliness is fellowship. Where is the best fellowship in the world? It's supposed to be the church fellowship—a fellowship centered in Jesus Christ.

Sometimes the most obvious things in life are the easiest to miss. One such thing is that if we say we believe in Jesus and are his followers, we are given to one another in love. We are called to a ministry of friendship. I didn't choose that ministry; it was *given* to me. I chose to be a follower of Jesus Christ, and my fellow Christians came with the bargain. That's the way it is. If you choose to be a follower of Jesus Christ, you get all the rest of us with him. We are all brothers and sisters in the family of God.

Freed by Grace

Early one morning, a few years ago, I was sitting in my study at the church, feeling rather lonely. The church had been struggling financially, and I was wondering if anybody was hearing the message of financial stewardship. Momentarily there was a knock at my door, and when I opened it, there stood a church member. This particular person had never before come to see me in all the years that I had been pastor. He wanted to tell me how much he appreciated me. He said, "This is your church. This is God's church. This is strange, but I want to have a prayer with you." For a few moments, he prayed for me. Then he shook my hand and left. He had been there only for a moment, but through that meaningful Christian fellowship with a church member who cared, my loneliness melted away.

In his own loneliness, Jesus went to three of his disciples, Peter, James, and John, and asked them to keep him company while he prayed through a troubling time. This is our model for true Christian community. "Everyone will know that you are my disciples," Jesus said, "if you have love for one another" (John 13:35).

We Can Replace Our Loneliness with an Active Friendship with God

Above all, loneliness should teach us to find a better friendship with God. What is loneliness, anyway? Basically, it is our homesickness for God. God has placed that longing in each of us. Augustine stated it this way: "Thou dost keep us restless, O God, until our hearts rest in Thee." As incredible as it sounds, the basic answer for our loneliness is *aloneness*—but aloneness *with God*. In this deliberately chosen aloneness, we cultivate our awareness of and our friendship with God. This is what Jesus was talking about when he advised, "When you pray, go into a room by yourself, shut the door and pray to your Father who is there in the secret place" (Matthew 6:6, NEB).

Years ago, my wife's mother had a brain tumor. After the first surgery, which had not been successful, I asked her if she had been afraid. "No," she said, "because as they were wheeling me down the hallway to surgery, I suddenly saw a picture in my mind of the Twenty-third Psalm." I thought deeply about my mother-in-law's remark. I know something about her devotional life: She honored Christ, and Christ honored her. She had an active friendship with God, and she knew that God was there for her during her time of great need. Ellsworth Kalas shares this story about the late Dr. Norman Vincent Peale.

[Dr.] Peale was passing through LaGuardia Airport several years ago en route to a speaking engagement. The agent, who knew him, also knew that Mrs. Peale often traveled with him. He said to Dr. Peale, "Traveling alone today, I see." "Yes," Dr. Peale answered, "I am traveling alone."

But as Dr. Peale moved away from the check-in counter, the man called after him, "You never travel alone." And Dr. Peale replied, "Nor do you." [3]

"You will leave me alone," said Jesus, "yet I am not alone because [God] is with me." Likewise, we are never truly alone when we walk with God.

Chapter 4   Worry

"Don't Worry"—
A Tall Order, Indeed!

"No one can serve two masters; for a slave will either hate the one and love the other, or be devoted to the one and despise the other. You cannot serve God and wealth.

"Therefore I tell you, do not worry about your life, what you will eat or what you will drink, or about your body, what you will wear. Is not life more than food, and the body more than clothing? Look at the birds of the air; they neither sow nor reap nor gather into barns, and yet your heavenly Father feeds them. Are you not of more value than they? And can any of you by worrying add a single hour to your span of life? And why do you worry about clothing? Consider the lilies of the field, how they grow; they neither toil nor spin, yet I tell you, even Solomon in all his glory was not clothed like one of these. But if God so clothes the grass of the field, which is alive today and tomorrow is thrown into the oven, will he not much more clothe you—you of little faith? Therefore do not worry, saying 'What will we eat?' or 'What will we drink?' or 'What will we wear?' For it is the Gentiles who strive for all these things; and indeed your heavenly Father knows that you need all these things. But strive first for the kingdom of God and his righteousness, and all these things will be given to you as well.

"So do not worry about tomorrow, for tomorrow will bring worries of its own. Today's trouble is enough for today."

Matthew 6:24-34

Think about the international arena: The Cold War between the United States and the former Soviet Union may be over, but will there ever be an end to the threat of nuclear weapons? Will the ever-growing world population finally explode in mass starvation and worldwide upheaval? Will there be any genuine cooperative reinvestment in the welfare of planet Earth?

Now look at the national scene: The economy has been on the upswing recently, but will it stay there, or come crashing down? What about our still-bloated national debt? our fading values? our struggling educational system? our unacceptably high crime rate? our lost idealism? our deterioration of family life? our growing disparity between the haves and the have-nots? our increasing emphasis on what separates us, rather than what brings us together? What is our future as a nation? Has the American Dream been forgotten?

And then there's our personal arena: Perhaps we are unhappy with our employment; or our relationships are shaky; or our debt is overwhelming; or our health is a problem; or we are getting older; or we are alone; or we are wondering if anybody will ever love us. Remember the movie *Born on the Fourth of July?* Tom Cruise portrayed real-life Vietnam veteran Ron Kovic, whose injuries suffered in the war had left him a paraplegic. Wasn't that a heart-rending cry when he screamed out in agony, "Who's ever going to love me?" His heart was so troubled by his condition and circumstance that he felt unlovable, and the pain and loneliness of that worry was too much.

So many of us are imprisoned in the haunting jails of excessive worry and its counterpart—fear. The penalty we pay is that we feel trapped in a joyless existence of dread and uneasiness.

In the midst of all this, we hear those strange words of Jesus from his Sermon on the Mount: "Do not worry about your life . . . (Matthew 6:25). "Lord, are you *serious*?" we ask. "We are only human, you know." But we can rest in full confidence that Jesus was quite serious when he spoke these words "Therefore I tell you," he said, "do not worry about your life."

We tend to forget that the word *therefore* is included. But it is of paramount importance. It is a connecting word. Jesus is connecting his thoughts of conquering excessive worry to our choosing God over *mammon*—the many facets of worldliness (money, success, fame, pride of possessions, and so forth). Putting God first in our lives brings worry or anxiety into line. Putting it another way, making God and

God's will our top priority and trusting God to provide for us is the answer to our human tendency toward excessive worry.

What *is* worry, anyway? Here is my definition: *Worry* is a sense of prolonged uneasiness that revolves around a thick center of fear. A highly nervous, insecure woman was heard remarking: "All of a sudden, I stopped worrying. And it worries me!" "Don't worry." Now *that's* a tall order, indeed! What makes worry such a struggle for us?

There's the Task of Worry

Many people in our time fail to distinguish between intelligent concern on the one hand and unbalanced concern on the other. Jesus does not say, "Take no thought for tomorrow," as one translation suggests. In reality, most of what Jesus said added up to the exact opposite of that. Taking thought for tomorrow is the very nature of discipleship.

Imagine where the church, or the nation, or an individual life would be if no thought was given to the future. Imagine where a marriage would be. At wedding ceremonies, I often share Jesus' parable of the man building a tower. Jesus said, "For which of you, intending to build a tower, does not first sit down and estimate the cost, to see whether [you have] enough to complete it?" (Luke 14:28, adapted). After sharing that passage, I usually list several of the costs of a good marriage—a commitment to permanency, the forsaking of all others, the nurturing of the relationship, an ever-maturing love, an understanding of forgiveness, and a commitment to God. At the wedding ceremony itself, I want the couple to be aware of Jesus' teaching and to take thought for their future. This is the only way they will succeed as a couple. In the Scripture, Jesus is not forbidding conscientious, sensible foresight. *Some* worry or anxiety about tomorrow is good and necessary. Jesus' words, "do not worry about tomorrow," are better understood as "do not be *distracted* by tomorrow."

In a recent year, I received a very newsy letter from a dear friend and colleague. A professor to the very end, he wrote these words in the last paragraph of his letter:

Before I close I feel I ought to give you a piece of advice. Maybe you are already doing it and it is not needed. Because you have this large *and* pivotal church as well as a regular TV audience, it is so very important that you schedule twenty hours each week in study, lest you become shallow, moralistic, and repetitious. Because of your position as spokesperson of the church, you need the study so that you will have a divine message for today's perplexed people. So, in signing off, God bless you and your preaching ministry.

What a wonderful reminder of "conscientious, sensible foresight or worry" for me or any other would-be preacher of the gospel of Jesus Christ. There are simply *some* things we *ought* to worry about. E.M. Forster, the novelist, said, "One has two duties—to be worried and not to be worried." When he pointed out that it is a duty to be worried, he was thinking about the needs of society and the obligation we have to take these needs to our hearts and consciences. There are simply some things we ought to be concerned about. God doesn't intend for us to live our lives without some worry or anxiety. Being a good citizen means being concerned for every citizen's good. Being a good parent means being concerned about the multiple needs of a child. Being a good churchperson always involves loving concern for the ministries of one's church.

In one of his books, Bishop Ernest Fitzgerald details a television interview he had seen in which "a highly respected American states-man was reflecting upon the people who had influenced his life most. He singled out an elementary schoolteacher whose name was unknown to listeners. 'She was kind but firm,' he said. 'Time after time she would hand back our homework with one sentence written across the top: "You can do better than this!" ' "[1]

Such is the task of worry. We can all do better than this. The right amount and the right kind of worry can help make us thoughtful, caring people. But the wrong kind, or *excessive* worry, can bind our hearts and our souls.

There's the Tension of Worry

Excessive worry is a disease of the spirit, and there are many who are afflicted by it. One of my favorite "Peanuts" comic strips shows Charlie Brown in the school nurse's office. As he waits, he observes: "So, here I am about to see the school nurse." Then Charlie Brown wonders: "She'll probably take my temperature and look down my throat . . . " Then he worries, "Maybe she'll take a blood sample. I hope she doesn't take a blood sample. Maybe she'll just weigh me." And finally, Charlie Brown agonizes, "If she mentions exploratory surgery, I'll scream!"

Such devastating worry often causes mental distress, physical discomfort, and spiritual numbness. When someone says, "I'm worried sick," that *might* not be an exaggeration. Excessive worry does make us sick. It causes tension headaches, skin rashes, stomach ulcers, heart attacks, nervous breakdowns, and a number of other related problems. Excessive worry frequently immobilizes us, makes us uptight, and alters our personality. It makes us feel restless, nervous, fearful, and overcome with dread. More often than not, it causes us to lose perspective. Take the husband who called his wife's obstetrician in the middle of the night to tell him her labor pains had begun. The physician asked, "Is this her first child?"

"No," replied the worried father-to-be, "this is her husband!"

Excessive worry also destroys the spiritual vitality of our lives. Actually, it is a form of agnosticism: If we worry excessively, it means that we question the very adequacy of God to meet our needs and the needs of others. In Matthew 6:24-34, Jesus is making the point that the God who cares for the birds of the air and the lilies of the field cares even more for humankind. He's asking each one of us, "Are you not of more value than they?" Excessive worry is such a pathetic indication of our lack of faith. It means that we do not believe that we have a God who loves us and is able to meet us at the point of our need. It means that we do not accept the biblical insistence that "God's grace is sufficient." And if that is the case, then no wonder we are worried. We *should* be, if we are facing life alone, with only our own wisdom and strength.

I read somewhere that more people take their lives in one particular month than in any other. (This information was based on the 37,000 suicides that occurred in the United States in a recent year.) Which month is it? It isn't January—the cold month. It's not March—the windy month. It is *May*—the month of beautiful flowers, fresh sunlight, and singing birds. The point was that excessive worry is a killer that respects neither the person involved nor the season of that person's life. For some, the tension of worry seems too great to overcome. But help is available.

There's the Treatment of Worry

Recall our definition of worry: *Worry* is a sense of prolonged uneasiness that revolves around a thick center of fear. So how do we deal with our excessive worry?

The words of Jesus come to us offering healing and hope. Jesus said, "Your heavenly Father knows that you need all these things. But strive first for the kingdom of God and his righteousness, and all these things will be given to you as well. So do not worry about tomorrow . . . " (Matthew 6:32b-34).

So what steps can you take for the treatment of excessive worry? Try the following:

1. Own your limitations. This means getting your thinking straight: Resign your position as CEO of the universe, effective immediately. You simply do not need to carry the weight of the world around on your back. None of us does; there are stronger hands available. This is part of what Jesus meant when he said, "Your heavenly Father knows . . . do not worry. . . . "

During a worship service I led on the Sunday after the Oklahoma City bombing tragedy, I became choked up and had to stop preaching for a moment. Afterward, a television interviewer asked me this question: "You are considered a man of strength by many. How would you explain [your emotional pause] today?"

I replied, "I really can't explain it. Some things are just close to your heart, human life, and freedom. I believe God uses the polished and the unpolished. Today was just one of those unpolished times, and I trust that God will use it."

2. *Get your priorities straight.* "Strive first for the kingdom of God and his righteousness," Jesus said (Matthew 6:33). Notice that Jesus spoke these words immediately following his warning against divided loyalty (6:24). Jesus is saying that the resolve of the heart or will is really the important thing in life. Too often we put the kingdom of God in second place. And having put ourself first, the result is that we are torn, troubled, anxious, and fearful. If there were less self-seeking, there would be far less worry.

In reality, Jesus is telling us to make our lives count for something important. This is borne out by a recent survey asking people ninety-five years old or older "what they'd do differently if they could live their lives over." Their responses: They'd reflect more: *What is the meaning of my life?*; they'd risk more; they'd do more things that will outlive them.[2] Jesus is telling us to make our lives count for something, and he wants us to do something about it *now.*

3. *Live one day at a time.* Jesus said, "Do not worry about tomorrow. . . . Today's trouble is enough for today (Matthew 6:34).

I will always remember the first time I went dove hunting. My uncle took me and some other friends to a large field. Then I was left by myself in a ditch with a shotgun and a box of shells. Within minutes, the sky was filled with doves. There was no way I could miss! I just blazed away, shooting into the sky. Of course, no dove fell. Finally, it dawned on me, when only a few doves remained flying by, that I had to *aim.* At that point, I aimed at one dove, then another, and got them. I succeeded in hunting only when I forgot about the rest of the covey and took aim at just one dove. So many people are worrying themselves to death over the rest of their lives when Jesus says, "Focus only on today."

4. *Count your blessings instead of your worries.* I read a magazine article somewhere about the power of self-talk. The writer discussed the advantages of holding an internal dialogue with yourself. She stressed replacing your *negative* self-talk with *positive* self-talk.

How does the old song go? "Count your many blessings, name them one by one, and it will surprise you, what the Lord has done."

"Don't Worry"—A Tall Order, Indeed!   41

We Can Trust in God and Act on Our Faith

In the final analysis, the best thing we can do about worry is to trust in God and act on our faith. I do not know of any other way to overcome excessive worry.

Years ago, a church member knocked on our parsonage door. After being admitted into the hall, he stood for a moment, as though searching for the right words to say. As his pastor, I waited. Then, he simply said, "Thanks for everything—I'm moving this week." I looked at the man, puzzled, searching my mind for anything I might have done to assist him; I could think of nothing. I told him so, and his response was one I will always remember: "You were always there if I needed you. It helped me so much to know that. If ever I had needed to knock on your door, you would have opened it to me."

In a much greater way, this is how Jesus described the fatherhood and motherhood of God—always there and caring, always providing and sustaining, and always faithful.

During World War I, the King of England sent a Christmas card to all the soldiers in the army. There was one soldier who had no friends or family. He received no Christmas presents. Then the royal Christmas card came. He thought to himself, "Even if no one else remembers me, my king does."

"Don't worry" is a tall order, indeed! But our Christ is of a taller order, and he remembers us—every one.

Chapter 5   Depression

On Top of the Blues

Ahab told Jezebel all that Elijah had done, and how he had killed all the prophets with the sword. Then Jezebel sent a messenger to Elijah, saying, "So may the gods do to me, and more also, if I do not make your life like the life of one of them by this time tomorrow." Then he was afraid; he got up and fled for his life, and came to Beersheba, which belongs to Judah; he left his servant there.

But he himself went a day's journey into the wilderness, and came and sat down under a solitary broom tree. He asked that he might die: "It is enough; now, O LORD, take away my life, for I am no better than my ancestors." Then he lay down under the broom tree and fell asleep. Suddenly an angel touched him and said to him, "Get up and eat." He looked, and there at his head was a cake baked on hot stones, and a jar of water. He ate and drank, and lay down again. The angel of the LORD came a second time, touched him, and said, "Get up and eat, otherwise the journey will be too much for you." He got up, and ate and drank; then he went in the strength of that food forty days and forty nights to Horeb the mount of God. At that place he came to a cave, and spent the night there.

Then the word of the LORD came to him, saying, "What are you doing here, Elijah?" He answered, "I have been very zealous for the LORD, the God of hosts; for the Israelites have forsaken your covenant, thrown down your altars, and killed your prophets with the sword. I alone am left, and they are seeking my life, to take it away.

He said, "Go out and stand on the mountain before the LORD, for the LORD is about to pass by." Now there was a great wind, so strong that it was splitting mountains and breaking rocks in pieces before the LORD, but the LORD was not in the wind; and after the wind an earthquake, but the LORD was not in the earthquake; and after the earthquake a fire, but the LORD was not in the fire; and after the fire a sound of sheer silence. When Elijah heard it, he wrapped his face in his mantle and went out and stood at the entrance of the cave. Then there came a voice to him that said, "What are you doing here, Elijah?" He answered, "I have been very zealous for the LORD, the God of hosts; for the Israelites have forsaken your covenant, thrown down your altars, and killed your prophets with the sword. I alone am left, and they are seeking my life, to take it away." Then the LORD said to him, "Go, return on your way to the wilderness of Damascus."

1 Kings 19:1-15a

Have you ever wondered why the feeling of low spirits is called "the blues"? *I* have! Blue is truly an awesome color. When I think of blue, I think of the beauty of a clear sky. I think of pretty blue eyes. I recall the song "My Blue Heaven." So it is difficult for me to connect blue with "the dumps."

Yet I recognize that the feeling of the blues is real. Who among us has not experienced them? Some of us may know the blues better than others know them, but we all know them. We all have our ups and downs, our smooth days and our rough days. Every one of us gets depressed at times. Every one of us serves time in the prison of his or her own personal version of the blues. Thomas A. Whiting shares this humorous story about one extraordinarily burdened man:

Two fellows were talking, and one asked the other, "How do you spend your income"? The other replied, "Thirty percent for housing, 30 percent for clothing, 40 percent for food, and 20 percent for recreation." The first man reacted, "That can't be! That's 120 percent!" The second responded, "Don't I know it!"[1]

Just what *are* "the blues," or *depression*? One dictionary defines *depression* as "sadness; gloominess; low spirits." Author and

Freed by Grace

physician M. Scott Peck describes depression as "the emotional side of despair. Cynicism is its intellectual side."[2] Whatever depression is, it gives us the feeling of being down. We are depressed when our emotions take control of us. We are depressed when we become the victims of our moods. Bodily illness can cause depression. A chemical imbalance can produce it. Inverted anger can bring it to life. Fatigue, grief, failure, loneliness, fear, guilt, rejection, indecision, joblessness, or tension—*all* have the potential to contribute to our being depressed.

Paul A. Hauck, a clinical psychologist, notes that there are three main causes of emotional depression. The first is *self-blame*. Sufferers hate themselves for doing things wrong. The second cause is *self-pity*. This is the belief that we do not deserve unfair treatment in this world. The third cause is *other-pity*—the belief that we should be terribly upset over other people's problems.[3] Whatever the cause of our depression, we need to deal with it honestly. And more often than not, we will need to deal with it in terms of confession, repentance, the acceptance of our forgiveness, and resolve.

Take a look at the First Book of Kings, chapter 19. The prophet Elijah was battling his own depression. His self-pity had forced both his mind and his heart to evacuate. He may have escaped the clutches of Ahab and Jezebel, but he was very much a prisoner of the blues.

Only a few hours earlier, on the top of Mount Carmel, Elijah had stood out as a giant among humankind. He had challenged the people of Israel and the 450 prophets of Baal with his magnificent declaration: "If the LORD is God, follow him" (1 Kings 18:21). Then he had put the prophets of Baal to the test, and Elijah and his God had emerged victorious. The prophets of Baal were then destroyed.

But soon thereafter, something happened that literally knocked the props out of Elijah's world. King Ahab returned and told his queen, Jezebel, of all that had taken place at Mount Carmel. Infuriated, Jezebel immediately sent a messenger to Elijah, telling him that she was going to have him killed. Rather than rising to the challenge, the Scripture says, Elijah was afraid, and he arose and ran for his life, despondent, discouraged, and in a terrible battle with the blues. But later, after Elijah encounters an angel, the symbol of God's presence,

God speaks to Elijah and offers him some valuable insights into dealing with his depression. It is these same insights that God would share with us today.

Look After Your Body

The first thing that God did for the depressed Elijah was something very practical: God allowed Elijah to get a good night's rest and then gave him something to eat. Note that God did not have the angel give Elijah a fresh vision or reinterpret the sacred writings or do some other phenomenal thing. God simply moved Elijah to do something very ordinary—to arise and eat.

So often it is our accelerated, hectic, hustle-and-bustle schedules that contribute to our depression. If our lifestyle is not conducive to good health, then more than likely we are abusing our body. The need is always for a balanced diet, proper rest, disciplined exercise, and regular consultation with a physician. We can hardly expect God to deliver us from the blues if we are constantly wiped out and exhausted. I haven't completely learned this lesson yet, but I am working on it.

In one magazine article, the author identified six signs that reveal that work has become an unhealthy obsession:

1. *No play.* You devote little or no time to play and even refuse to take vacations. . . .
2. *Trying too hard.* Work makes you anxious and tense. Nothing you produce at the office seems good enough. . . .
3. *Body revolt.* Your punishing regimen drives your body to fight back. You feel fatigued but find it impossible to relax. . . .
4. *One-track life.* You don't have much of a social or love life. . . .
5. *One-track mind.* Your single-minded dedication to work is causing interpersonal problems. . . .
6. *Martyrdom.* You view work as torture and yourself as a martyr. . . . [4]

Well, are *we* workaholics? What would those around us say? God was so concerned that Elijah take care of his body that God actually sent him on a retreat, a vacation. Only after God dealt with Elijah's physical needs did God deal with Elijah's depression.

Look after your body.

Remember That Your Present Mood Is Only Temporary

People in Texas tend to talk about the weather there. They say, "If you don't like it, wait a minute, it'll change." This is also the nature of depression. No matter how you feel right now, wait a minute. You may presently reside in the midst of a storm, but behind the storm is the calm. Your present mood is only temporary.

Consider Elijah. Here was a man of God who dared to defy the wickedness of King Ahab and Queen Jezebel. Elijah, by the power of God, brought about a drought that lasted three-and-a-half years. Because of his faith, he was able to provide a widow with a container of oil and a jar of flour that never diminished. Because of Elijah's faith, God raised the widow's son from the dead. Through Elijah, God sent fire down from heaven and destroyed the 450 prophets of Baal.

Yet with all that power, we also know that Elijah was human. Consequently, we find him sitting under a juniper tree and praying to die (1 Kings 19:4). The elation of his physical and spiritual victories had passed, and the strain had left him depressed and afraid. "Take away my life," he pleaded. Here is Elijah, great hero of God, completely down and out and suffering from the blues. But if you read further, you will see that Elijah doesn't stay that way; his mood is only temporary!

We too can take comfort in the fact that life moves in cycles. At times we are up, and at other times we are down. All normal living takes its toll and sometimes leaves us with the blues. But take note: To have the blues does not mean that God has deserted us. To have the blues does not mean that we are faithless. Rather, to have the blues simply means that we are human and we are participating in the normalcy of life.

I remember one year when I served as chaplain of the high school football team that had zero wins and ten losses. I was also the "color man" on the radio for that team. As you can imagine, there is just so much color for an 0-10 team. I never prayed so many "losing" prayers as I did for that team. Likewise, I never offered as many excuses over the radio as I did for that team. Before that season was over, *all* of us had the blues—coaches, players, principal, fans, radio announcer—

even me. But by the time spring football practice rolled around, we were all excited all over again.

Remember that your present mood is only temporary.

Share It with Somebody

A friendly mail carrier paused at the door for a moment to chat with a little four-year-old boy about the boy's baby sister. The mail carrier asked the boy, "Can she talk?"

"No," the little boy answered. "She has her teeth, but her words haven't come in yet."

If we have our words, we should share our depression with somebody. Elijah was given the opportunity to talk about his depression—to "clear the air." His answer to God's question—"What are you doing here?"—was simple. Elijah explained that he was despondent and had left his post of duty because he alone had remained faithful to God, and now his life was in danger. Evidently, he felt that God too had forsaken him.

All of us need to share our depression with somebody—*somebody,* not everybody. If we attempt to share it with everybody, then before long, people will run in the opposite direction when they see us coming. But it *is* important to face our depression with some trusted, wholesome listener. That's how we get our depression out into the open. That's how we learn about the causes, and not just the symptoms. That's how we gain some new perspective about overcoming depression.

And it is even more important to share our depression with God. Our whole spirituality is based upon the premise that there is a God and that God cares. We take our cue from Jesus. Jesus always took his concerns to his heavenly Father—even his concerns of anguish. Think about Jesus' prayers in Gethsemane and Bethany. In Gethsemane, he prayed in great agony, and in Bethany, he prayed in sorrow for Lazarus, his deceased friend. The result of those prayers was great power.

Herb Miller shares this story about the late Harry Emerson Fosdick, pastor of Riverside Church in New York City: "[Fosdick] was standing by the rail admiring Niagara Falls. The man next to him said, 'You know, right there is the greatest unused power in all the world.'

Fosdick replied, 'No, I'm afraid I'll have to disagree with you. The greatest unused power in all the world is prayer!' "[5]
Share it with somebody. Start with the Lord.

Renew Your Relationship with God

The most important thing God did for Elijah in order to enable him to rise above his depression was to give Elijah a fresh vision of who God was and is.

Elijah expected God to come in the wind, the earthquake, and the fire, ways God had used in the past. But God didn't come that way this time. Reeling from the blues, Elijah probably wondered whether God was going to come to him at all. And then it happened: Elijah heard "a still small voice" (1 Kings 19:12, RSV). God confirmed God's presence in Elijah's insight and imagination. Putting it another way, God worked an inside job and brought Elijah peace and power.

Regardless of our circumstances, Christ comes to us bringing forgiveness, confidence, hope, purpose, and power. Christ comes to deliver us from our depression. Like Elijah, you too can renew your relationship with God.

Do Something for Somebody Else

It has been said that the duty of a college president is to speak and not to think; the duty of the faculty is to think and not to speak; and the duty of the dean is to keep the president from speaking and the faculty from thinking. That's not exactly what I had in mind by doing something for somebody else!

God doesn't come to us for free. God didn't come to Elijah for free: God had assignments for him. In the midst of Elijah's depression, God sent him back into the world to be a prophet and to help others.

I am so grateful that God doesn't give up on us when we have the blues! What if God said to us, "Because you have the blues, you are tainted. I have no further use for you." That would truly be devastating. On the contrary, God calls all of us to renewed service. God knows that as we involve ourselves in service to God and others, our blues will melt away.

On occasion, I will go into a hospital room where a child is ill. It might be eight or nine o'clock in the evening. I'll ask the child's mother if she has had any dinner. Usually, the reply will be no. Then I might ask if she has had any lunch. Again the answer is no. What happens is that this mother gets so involved in the needs of her child that she forgets all about her own needs.

Dealing with the blues is like parents who are trying to put together a Christmas toy for their child. The toy just won't fit together properly. Then one parent finally spots a sticker on one of the pieces that reads, "If all else fails, read the directions!" When we're dealing with the blues, we should read the directions *first:*

> Look after your body.
> Remember that your present mood is only temporary.
> Share it with somebody.
> Renew your relationship with God.
> Do something for somebody else.

Why Did God Take My Mama?

His disciples said, "Yes, now you are speaking plainly, not in any figure of speech! Now we know that you know all things, and do not need to have anyone question you; by this we believe that you came from God." Jesus answered them, "Do you now believe? The hour is coming, indeed it has come, when you will be scattered, each one to his home, and you will leave me alone. Yet I am not alone because the Father is with me. I have said this to you, so that in me you may have peace. In the world you face persecution. But take courage; I have conquered the world!"

John 16:29-33

I had concluded the funeral service, and he just sat there staring into space. His wife and children were gathered around him, desperately trying to lend their support. He must have been in his early fifties, and he was totally distraught over the death of his mother.

This man was literally held captive by grief. Finally, he managed to walk with his wife out into the cemetery. After a few moments, I eased up behind him and put my hand on his shoulder. Amidst his sobbing, he asked, "Why did God take my mama? She loved life. I don't like God."

I replied, "I really don't have an answer to your question. But I do believe that God is in this with you because of God's love experienced through the cross of Christ. And God understands your anger, and it's all right." Questions such as the one this man asked lead us to focus on the important matters of grief, reaction to grief, and grace.

Grief is a sober subject, and yet, as Tennyson put it, "Never morning wore to evening, but some heart did break." In looking for hope through our despair—light upon our darkness—consider these words of Jesus: "In the world you face persecution. But take courage; I have conquered the world!" (John 16:33*b*). Another translation puts it this way: "In the world you have tribulation; but be of good cheer, I have overcome the world" (RSV).

Jesus is suggesting several things here that will help us deal with grief, reaction to grief, and grace.

Jesus Is Telling Us That Grief Is an Equal Opportunity Employer, and We Must Accept It

There are many forms of grief—divorce, job loss, the threat of job loss, moving, physical disabilities, young people leaving home, hospitalization, failure, retirement, imprisonment—and the list is endless. *Grief* has been defined by Dr. Wayne Oates, one of America's best-known counselors, as "the aftermath of any deeply significant loss."[1] But here, we will concentrate specifically on the ultimate grief.

The telephone rings or someone comes to the door. The message is one we hoped we'd never hear: Someone we dearly love is dead. I distinctly remember being picked up at the Harwell Avenue Grammar School in La Grange, Georgia, when I was a child. I was ten years old and was told by a family friend, "Your mother is dead." That was years ago, but I will always remember the devastation I felt.

I also recall a telephone conversation I had early one morning in 1977. My sister called and said that my father had died during the night. I remember the feeling of disconnection.

But since death is a common experience, some form of this message comes to all of us at some time or another in our lives. It comes to the young and the older, the haves and the have-nots, the ready and the unready. Not a single one of us is exempt.

Supposedly there is a tombstone somewhere in Indiana, more than a hundred years old, and on it are written these lines:

Pause, stranger, when you pass me by.
As you are now, so once was I.

As I am now, so will you be.
So prepare for death and follow me.

A humorist is said to have passed that way and added two lines that seem rather light, but actually have vital and serious meaning:

To follow you I'm not content,
Until I know which way you went.

Sorrow, loss, and grief simply cannot be escaped. If we live long enough, we will experience grief.

In her book *Where the Wind Begins,* Paula D'Arcy, who lost her husband and child in a traffic accident, says that "within deep joy, within its essence, is also the possibility of deep sorrow. And only fools, those who fool themselves, think they can open their arms to embrace one without the other. They cannot be separated."[2] There is a false way of looking at things, one in which we believe that life should be all sweetness and roses, that anything that disturbs our happiness is unreal and shouldn't be there.

Jesus, however, was not fooled by any such distortion of the truth. He looked at things as they really were and saw that in the kind of world in which we live, trouble or grief is inevitable. He said it as plainly as possible. "In the world you have tribulation" (trouble, death, grief)—period. There is no way to avoid it.

And this is what the writer of Ecclesiastes meant by these words: "For everything there is a season, and a time for every matter under heaven: . . . a time to weep, and a time to laugh; / a time to mourn, and a time to dance" (3:1, 4). If laughing and dancing are a part of life, so are weeping and mourning.

Jesus Is Telling Us That We Should Seek to Understand the Nature of the Grief Experience

If you have experienced grief, you will undoubtedly remember it. If you haven't, consider the following reality. Your body is fatigued, and your emotions are "on edge." Your heart is breaking, and you are sure your life is ruined. You are confused and disconnected. You wander around aimlessly trying to get it together, but you can't concentrate. At times, you feel as though you are going to suffocate. You even have difficulty breathing. Your emotions are mixed. You feel betrayal, loneliness, fear, gratitude, guilt, anger, and self-pity. At intervals, you wonder if you are losing your mind. You doubt that anyone else has ever felt the way you feel.

What is grief? Doug Manning, in his book *Comforting Those Who Grieve,* says that *grief* is "the natural response to any loss. The key word is that it is *natural.* There is an orderly process people go through in dealing with grief. This process is nature's way of healing a broken heart."[3]

In some respects, the grief process is similar to the healing process when a person breaks a bone. There are no shortcuts or magical cures for healing. Rather, the bone has to go through the natural process to heal. And so does a person who is grieving.

After the loss of his mother, the writer Henri Nouwen said, "I had to fight the temptation to 'get back to normal' too soon."[4] How long does the grief process take? It varies, but some who know say that it lasts anywhere from two years to four years; sometimes longer, sometimes shorter—but two years is about average. This means that the grief process usually lasts much longer than most people think, and it is full of peaks and valleys.

In 1992, actor Tony Randall lost his wife of fifty-four years, Florence, to cancer. The two had even been college sweethearts. In a 1995 interview, Tony said that "work has helped me to cope with the death of my wife three years ago. Work is the only therapy and the best therapy. After her death, I really didn't have time to grieve. But if I'm by myself and just sit down, it'll come over me in waves." Whether he realized it or not, Tony Randall was still very much involved in the grieving process, even three years later.

Wayne Oates lists the various stages of grief as follows:

Stage 1: Shock. That's when you first get the news: "I can't believe it."

Stage 2: Numbness. In a dazed condition, "you try to absorb the shock." You attend only to the practical necessities of the funeral.

Stage 3: Belief and Disbelief. This is the struggle between fantasy and reality. During sleep you may dream that the deceased is alive. Then the dream awakens you, and you know it isn't so. *Stage 4: Depression [or Acceptance of Reality].* This is the time of mourning "when you can [cry] without control or shame." *Stage 5: Selective Memory.* "You get along quite well until a fresh reminder of your loss re-presents the whole issue." Perhaps you will see someone you haven't seen since the funeral. This may remind you all over again. But this is a short-lived condition, and you soon return to a more even emotional control. *Stage 6: Commitment [or Recovery].* You commit yourself "to start living again and rebuilding your life."[5] You begin to understand what Paul meant when he said, "Grieve, but not as people who have no hope."

Something of these stages occurs in nearly every kind of grief. But this progression is not always clearly defined. The griever may go into shock, progess into suffering, regress back into shock, then into suffering again, and so on. We need to keep in mind that the grief process is jagged, never smooth. But it *does* lead to recovery.

Jesus Is Telling Us That, in Spite of It All, to "Be of Good Cheer, I Have Overcome the World"

Listen carefully to the words of Jesus (from the RSV): "In the world you have tribulation; but be of good cheer, I have overcome the world" (John 16:33*b*). We know something about suffering and sadness and grief and tribulation. But Jesus doesn't stop there. He goes on and says this other thing: "But be of good cheer, I have overcome the world." How could Jesus say that? The answer is found in the preceding verse. "Yet," says Jesus, "I am not alone because the Father is with me" (John 16:32).

So where can we go to find the strength we need to face life, death, and grief? We cannot find the strength we need by looking back at the sorrows of the past and asking why. In the Old Testament, Job didn't find the answer there. Job found the answer in the whirlwind when he was encountered by God.

After hearing of the drowning of his son in the Rio Grande River, Bob Buford was walking along the bluff of that river, "as frightened as I've ever felt." He said to himself, *"Here's something you can't dream your way out of. . . . Here's something you can't think your way out of, buy your way out of, or work your way out of. . . . [Here is] something you can only trust your way out of."*[6]

Sometimes God's best gift to us is simply the strength to endure, and the knowledge that we do not have to do it alone. As Paul said, "For I am convinced that neither death, nor life, . . . nor anything else in all creation, will be able to separate us from the love of God in Christ Jesus our Lord" (Romans 8:38). We will face grief in our lives, but with the goodness of God, Jesus tells us, we can get through it.

Finally, Jesus Would Have Us Look at Some of the Practical Ways We Can Deal with Our Grief

We do these things in the full knowledge and faith of the one who said, "Be of good cheer, I have overcome the world."

We can remember the Resurrection. M. Scott Peck said, "Never in my wildest imagination have I thought that I could beat [death]. Even Jesus didn't beat it. All he did was painfully hang around for a little bit in an ethereal, barely recognizable form to make a point. The point of resurrection is not that we can beat death; it is that there is more to us than our death, than our mere bodies."[7] Our loved ones are in a better place.

We can refrain from brooding. Though I have lost both my parents, a stepmother, and several of my best friends, this does not qualify me as an authority on grief. But I do know this: We can cultivate our grief by brooding on it, and it will master our lives.

We can keep tending to our spiritual disciplines. When I received the heavy news that my father had died, for several days I didn't feel like spending quiet time. But I kept to my discipline of quiet time anyway, and from it I received an added source of strength.

We can stay involved in fellowship with others. If we are effectively dealing with our grief, we will undoubtedly become more sensitive to the needs of others.

We can take some definite course of action. When King David was caught up in his grief over the loss of his child, he took a bath, cleaned up, and went to the Temple. Then he ate. That sounds like our Sunday routine. Such routines can help us when we are unable to concentrate or focus.

We can trust God. Max Lucado, in his book *A Gentle Thunder,* shares this story:

> Several years ago I heard then Vice President George Bush speak at a prayer breakfast. He told of his trip to Russia to represent the United States at the funeral of Leonid Brezhnev. The funeral was . . . precise and stoic. . . . No tears were seen, and no emotion displayed. With one exception. Mr. Bush told how Brezhnev's widow was the last person to witness the body before the coffin was closed. For several seconds she stood at his side and then reached down and performed the sign of the cross on her husband's chest.
>
> In the hour of her husband's death, she went not to Lenin, not to Karl Marx, not to Khrushchev. In the hour of death she turned to a Nazarene carpenter who had lived two thousand years ago and who dared to claim: "Don't let your hearts be troubled. Trust in God, and trust in me."[8]

Jesus said, "In the world you have tribulation [grief]; but be of good cheer [take courage], I have overcome the world." Amen. So let it be.

Down, But Not Out

He left that place and came to his hometown, and his disciples followed him. On the sabbath he began to teach in the synagogue, and many who heard him were astounded. They said, "Where did this man get all this? What is this wisdom that has been given to him? What deeds of power are being done by his hands! Is not this the carpenter, the son of Mary and brother of James and Joses and Judas and Simon, and are not his sisters here with us?" And they took offense at him. Then Jesus said to them, "Prophets are not without honor, except in their hometown, and among their own kin, and in their own house." And he could do no deed of power there, except that he laid his hands on a few sick people and cured them. And he was amazed at their unbelief.

Mark 6:1-6a

Ever been discouraged? *Sure* you have. We all have. At some time or other, all of us have been held captive by the enslaving power of discouragement.

Most of us are people of great expectation. Seldom, however, does the expectation match the reality. Consequently, our anticipation is imprisoned, and we become discouraged. This message is for anyone who is tempted to say, "I'm sorry for me."

Not long ago, a four-year-old girl came to my wife, her teacher, feeling discouraged.

She said, "Mrs. Brady, Susie's calling me names."

My wife responded, "Well, what did she call you?"

The little girl replied, "A *bit*. She called me a *bit*."

My wife asked, "Well, what is a *bit*?"

The little girl answered, "Well, I don't know what it is . . . but I know I don't *like* it."

Jesus Christ lived a life of perfection, but there were times when things went wrong, even for *him*. There were times when he too was tempted to say, "I'm sorry for me." But he didn't. By following Jesus' example in our times of discouragement, we too can discover our own route to freedom.

As Jesus turned toward his hometown of Nazareth, his heart must have been filled with great expectation and excitement. He had just come through several absolutely spectacular days: He had stilled a storm, cast demons out of a madman, cured a woman of cancer, and raised a little girl from the dead! To be sure, he was looking forward to the thrill of going home. He was looking forward to the joy of visiting with family and friends. And, in addition, he was certain that they would be ready to receive God's message through him.

Not long ago, I had the privilege of preaching four days in my hometown. It was such a special joy to have the opportunity to visit with my family and old friends. With the exception of setting off the burglar alarm in my sister's house one afternoon, summoning the police, it was a spectacularly fantastic visit. And the opportunity to preach in my home church was quite a treat. There's nothing quite like the joy of knowing that God has used you to do good in your own hometown.

But tragically, Jesus did not experience this kind of joy when he entered his hometown synagogue in Nazareth and began to teach. He discovered that his message was so challenging and inspiring that the people were shocked. They said: "Where did this man get all this? . . . Is not this the carpenter, the son of Mary and brother of James and Joses and Judas and Simon, and are not his sisters here with us?" (Mark 6:2b-3a). In other words, "Isn't his family rather ordinary? How can he possibly claim to represent the Almighty?" The people were offended at him.

It is almost impossible to imagine the heartache that Jesus must have felt as he walked into his hometown to find that the people he so loved didn't understand him. But these people not only didn't understand him or accept his message, they actually expressed hostility and even contempt for him. Jesus' morale must have been at a low ebb. He must certainly have faced the captivity of discouragement.

What did Jesus do in the face of such discouragement? What did he do when he was tempted to say, "I'm sorry for me"?

Jesus Refused to Quit

The late Hubert Humphrey, vice president of the United States under Lyndon Johnson, waged a courageous battle against cancer. During the height of Humphrey's illness, he wrote: "The biggest mistake people make is giving up. Adversity is an experience, not a final act. Some people look upon setback as the end. They are always looking for the benediction rather than the invocation."[1]

Jesus was not one of those "benediction" people. For in the midst of his discouragement, he refused to quit. Jesus refused to give up. He did not see in his discouragement a hopeless situation. Consequently, he did not lose his perspective or zeal for the greater purposes of God. Instead, he continued on with his ministry.

One of my favorite Old Testament books is the Book of Psalms. Literally, the Psalms deal with every conceivable human emotion and mood. One moment the psalmist is upbeat, full of faith and hope. The next moment, the psalmist is down, full of doubt and despair. Another moment, the psalmist is offering praise and thanksgiving; the next, he is complaining in dread and discouragement. No matter how we feel at any given moment of our lives, the psalmist speaks *to* and *for* us. Look at Psalm 18. The psalmist says, "By you I can crush a troop, / and by my God I can leap over a wall" (verse 29). The psalmist is saying that there is nothing too discouraging for me if I am connected to God. This was also the position and experience of Jesus. The message is, "Don't quit." Life may be hard, but it is never impossible, and we can make it if we try.

Recall for a moment Captain Scott O'Grady, the young American military pilot whose plane was shot down over war-torn Bosnia. He spent six days subsisting on nothing but bugs and rainwater, and he was finally rescued by a courageous group of young marines. Upon being shot down, O'Grady could have become discouraged and given up. He was going against unbelievable odds that he would ever make it back alive. Later, when asked how Captain O'Grady had made it, Admiral Leighton Smith, Commander of NATO forces in Southern Europe, said that O'Grady had managed to survive because he is "very smart and very determined and very gutsy."[2] O'Grady had not let discouragement get him down; he had simply refused to quit.

Suppose Jesus had quit that day he came home to Nazareth, or later when he was condemned to die at Calvary. In spite of the darkness and discouragement he must have felt, Jesus walked on to Calvary with an unfaltering faith. Like Scott O'Grady, he drew on a power beyond himself.

There is not a whole lot God can do with quitters. But there are unlimited possibilities for the one who will walk out into the darkness with his or her hand in the hand of God.

Jesus Sought to Be an Asset Anyway

The writer of Mark says, "And [Jesus] could do no deed of power there, except that he laid his hands on a few sick people and cured them" (6:5). Jesus was severely limited in Nazareth. He was limited because of the people's unbelief. Evidently, he had never seen such unbelief. We are told in the text that he actually "was amazed" at it (verse 6). But rather than giving up in the face of this overwhelming discouragement and feeling sorry for himself, Jesus sought to be an asset anyway. He laid his hands upon a few sick persons and healed them. What a blessing he must have been to those few sick folks! In the midst of his discouragement, Jesus looked for and found a way to do some good.

I saw a movie on television called *Past the Bleachers*. It's the story of a young couple who has lost their only son. The father has much difficulty accepting his son's death. He sees his son's face in practically every child. The father is living in limbo, gripped by his grief and discouragement.

One day a wise community leader approaches him about coaching a Little League team. After much thought and discussion with his wife, he decides to do it. What is the result of this father's decision? He helps

　　　　　　　　　　　　　　　　　　　　Freed by Grace

his community and the children by coaching the team. He befriends a lonely older man and makes him his assistant coach. And he and his wife wind up adopting one of the children on the team, a boy who cannot speak, who needed parents even as they needed a child. The man had sought to be an asset anyway, despite his setback, and he was. Think about Paul and Silas (Acts 16:16-40). They were in a jail cell. Do you think they stopped preaching until their crisis was over and they could get out of jail? No! They preached right there in the jail cell. The next thing you know, they've turned that cell into a revival meeting and have baptized the Philippian jailer and his family. Paul and Silas sought to be an asset anyway.

Jesus Lived in the Confidence of God's Presence and Trusted the Rest to God

When Jesus had done what he could in Nazareth, he moved on and continued the task God had given him. When we've done all we can about our discouragement, we too can move on and trust the rest to God. As the psalmist affirmed, "It is for you, O LORD, that I wait" (38:15). A willingness to trust our discouragement to God will usually mean that we have arrived at several basic assumptions about life:

1. Our impossibility may be God's possibility. A few years ago, when my wife, Myron, and I were in Boston, we went by Old Trinity Church. This was the church where the great preacher Phillips Brooks served. Phillips Brooks was such a powerful force for God that later the church members built a statue of him that still stands in front of the church. God used Phillips Brooks in a mighty way as a minister of the gospel. But did you know that Phillips Brooks actually dreamed of being a teacher? In fact, he had started out to be a teacher, but as a teacher, he was a complete failure. God had made other plans for Phillips Brooks and provided the means for him to become a success. What can we learn from this? Simply, let our impossibility become God's possibility. We may not know what plans God has for us in our lives, but *God* does. When one thing won't work, usually, something else will.

2. *You can take the next step.* No matter how discouraging life may become, there is always something we can do about it, if we only will. God never deserts us. God promised Joshua, and God promises us, "As I was with Moses, so I will be with you; I will not fail you or forsake you" (Joshua 1:5).

Whatever it is, we can take the next step.

3. *There is absolutely nothing that God and we cannot handle together.* And, of course, this includes overcoming our discouragement. The psalmist put it forcefully—and correctly—in Psalm 37:5 when he said: "Commit your way to the LORD; / trust in him, and he will act."

When There's More to Fear Than Fear Itself

On that day, when evening had come, he said to them, "Let us go across to the other side." And leaving the crowd behind, they took him with them in the boat, just as he was. Other boats were with him. A great windstorm arose, and the waves beat into the boat, so that the boat was already being swamped. But he was in the stern, asleep on the cushion; and they woke him up and said to him, "Teacher, do you not care that we are perishing?" He woke up and rebuked the wind, and said to the sea, "Peace! Be still!" Then the wind ceased, and there was a dead calm. He said to them, "Why are you afraid? Have you still no faith?" And they were filled with great awe and said to one another, "Who then is this, that even the wind and the sea obey him?"

Mark 4:35-41

The level of fear in this country escalated one hundred percent on April 19, 1995, the day of the terrible tragedy in Oklahoma City—the bombing of the Alfred P. Murrah Federal Building. Oklahoma City is in the heartland of the United States of America. Terrorists acts occur in other parts of the world, but not in the United States. Not in the heartland. Perhaps it was on April 19, 1995, that we in the United States realized anew just how vulnerable we all are.

Two weeks after the Oklahoma City incident, I was invited to speak at a volunteer-recognition ceremony for the U.S. Department of Education in the federal building in Dallas. As I stepped out of the elevator and onto the first floor of the federal building, I saw a large contingent of security persons. Everyone coming and going had to be identified and was being carefully scrutinized. Sign-in and sign-out sheets were being closely monitored. Nametags were highly visible. The atmosphere was tense and fearful. I felt a twinge of fear myself as I entered the building. But I was only going to be there for a couple of hours. Consequently, I could not help but wonder about the lurking fear that must have been in the hearts of all those who worked there.

Whether it pertains to the Oklahoma City tragedy, an approaching tornado, a serious illness, or something else, fear is ever present. So many persons are serving time in the various prisons of fear.

Over a generation ago, a British publisher asked several laypersons to write some sermons to be published under the title "If I Could Preach Only Once." Among those invited to write was the late Gilbert Chesterton, a noted English journalist and author. "If I had only one sermon to preach," wrote Chesterton, "it would be a sermon against fear."

That was a wise choice then, and it is also a wise choice today. In the light of modern human need, I believe that Jesus Christ authorizes this sort of message; indeed, I believe that he *encourages* it.

You will remember that it was President Franklin Delano Roosevelt who pointed out the destructive power of fear when he said, "The only thing we have to fear is fear itself." While that's inarguably a memorable quote, simply fearing fear will not enable us to disarm it. There are some basic characteristics of fear that we should all be aware of if we hope to recognize it and deal with it in a constructive, positive way.

Fear Is Real and Can Overcome Us

Obviously, not all fears are destructive. There are some fears that can be labeled "good" fears. The cultivation of these fears enables us and our loved ones to survive and move forward in life. We parents should teach our children to be afraid of some things—containers marked "poison," the careless use of matches, speeding automobiles, and so forth. These are legitimate fears, and they are absolutely essential to the good life or life at all.

In addition, some fears are good in the sense that they provide us with strength we didn't know we had. Dr. Lawrence LaCour, former professor of preaching at Oral Roberts Seminary, told of a woman whose teenage son became trapped under his automobile. While changing a tire, the automobile had slipped off the jack and pinned the boy to the ground. Upon hearing his agony, the boy's mother raced to his rescue and single-handedly lifted the automobile, freeing her son. When asked later by a reporter how she managed to lift the automobile by herself, she replied, "I love my son; he was threatened, and I'm responsible. This is my son." Indeed, there are times when fear is good.

Most of us spend far too much of our lives being afraid—not of the types of "good" fears mentioned above, but rather of *destructive* fears. These fears tend to warp life, paralyze it, or even destroy it. They rob life of its energy and joy. Among these destructive fears are the fears of rejection, losing control, being inadequate, failing, pain, dying, the unknown, being betrayed, being helpless, being hurt, or a loved one's being hurt.

A few years ago, our youngest son, along with four of his friends, stopped for gas near Hillsboro, Texas. Our son was standing outside the gas station when a man being chased by the police suddenly grabbed him, put a knife to his throat, and held him hostage. The incident ended tragically: The assailant was killed by police while still holding the knife at our son's throat. Shortly after the ordeal, my wife and I were talking about our son, and I remember saying to her, "Sometimes I'd just like to close the door and keep him inside." But as we both agreed, that was destructive fear speaking. To keep our son hidden away from the world—even with the good intention of keeping him safe from harm— would have been an attempt to "play God" and would have violated his freedom as a developing child of God. The love we learn from Christ is never possessive love. Sometimes Christ's call to us as parents is not only to serve, but to relax.

Pastor Frank L. Fowler III describes the scenario of one man's conversation with God upon entering into heaven. When the man, Mr. Smith, comes to the head of the line, God greets him and asks him to tell about his life. In an attempt to impress, Mr. Smith points out that he was a good person, was always kind to others, went to church once in a while, and even served on a committee. Thinking he has pleased the Lord, Mr. Smith proudly adds that he always gave his neighbor leftovers from his tomato garden. Then it is God's turn to speak:

"Mr Smith, why didn't you refuse to go along with the unethical business deals at work?"
Mr. Smith replies, "I was afraid I'd lose my job."
"Why didn't you do any more to help the hungry and sick children of the world?" asked the Creator.
"I was afraid my family wouldn't have enough," says Mr. Smith.
"Why didn't you go to your neighbors when their home was breaking up and offer to help?"
... "I was afraid they'd think I was prying."
God's response to all this is, "Mr. Smith, you spent far too much of your life being afraid."[1]

Elizabeth O'Connor, in her book *Cry Pain, Cry Hope,* described a sermon she heard on fear. She quoted the preacher:

"When I reflect on my life and what I really want, it is not to be afraid. When I am afraid, I am miserable. I play it safe. I restrict myself. I hide the talent of one in the ground. I am not deeply alive—the depths of me are not being expressed. When I am afraid, a tiny part of me holds captive most of me which rebels against the tyranny of the minority. When I am afraid, I am a house divided against itself. So more than anything else, I want to be delivered from fear. . . ."[2]

It is this kind of paralyzing fear that the passage in Mark describes. As evening was descending, Jesus felt the need to cross over to the other side of the Sea of Galilee. (We are not told *why* Jesus wanted to go to the other side; he just *did.*) Exhausted from his rigorous teaching schedule, Jesus fell asleep in the boat. It was at this point that the storm hit.

Though sudden storms on the Sea of Galilee were not unusual, they were terrifying, to say the least. So while Jesus was sleeping, the disciples were struggling to keep the boat in the water. They were doing all they could, fighting the unruly winds and waves, but it just wasn't enough. The boat was filling with water and sinking, and things were out of control. The fact that the disciples' fear was real and was

Freed by Grace

about to overcome them is apparent from their awakening Jesus, and from their question to him: "Teacher, do you not care that we are perishing?"

There are times when we feel as those disciples felt—that the storm is so big, and our boats are so small. No matter what we do, our efforts seem inadequate. "Teacher, do you not care that we are perishing?" Fear is real and can overcome us.

Fear Is Overcome When Faith Is Placed in the Presence

As the storm was slashing against the boat, with the disciples fearing for their lives, they did the only thing they could do: They called upon the Master, their Teacher, for help.

Centuries before, the psalmist had testified, "The LORD is my light and salvation; / whom shall I fear? / The LORD is the stronghold of my life; / of whom shall I be afraid?" Psalm 27, of which these two verses are a part, is a psalm of trust. The psalmist acknowledges his reliance on God.

The Scripture says, "[Jesus] woke up and rebuked the wind, and said to the sea, 'Peace! Be still!' Then the wind ceased, and there was a dead calm" (Mark 4:39). Those three words, "Peace! Be Still!" say enough. The one speaking here has all the authority. Jesus is in control of the situation.

But we do an injustice to this passage if we merely interpret it in a literal sense. If this story describes simply a physical miracle in which an actual storm was stilled, then it is a magnificent story, but nonetheless it is something that happened once and that cannot happen again. In this case, it is irrelevant to us. But if we read it in a *symbolic* sense, it is far more valuable and meaningful, for when the disciples actually *trusted* Jesus, the storm became a calm, a peace.

Some time ago, a friend telephoned me, long distance. I could tell that he was not in his usual good mood. He said he had called for two reasons. One, he wanted to get on my church's sermon mailing list. And two, he had a brain tumor. My friend went on to say that he was undergoing radiation treatment. In response, I assured him that he would be remembered in prayer. I affirmed his taking of the radiation treatment and encouraged him to trust in the Higher Power. A few months later, my friend died, but he died in complete peace. As he trusted in the Higher Power, his storm became a calm. The only truly effective way to get rid of our fears is to give them to God. Take a close look at what Jesus said to the disciples. He said to them, "Why are you afraid? Have you still no faith?" (verse 40). In other words, Jesus was asking his disciples why they didn't trust what they believed. That's essentially the same question Jesus asks us today: Why are you so fearful? Why are you afraid? When will you learn to trust what you believe?

What are some of the things that we, as Christians, believe about God?

1. We believe that God loves us with an enduring love.

2. We believe that God believes in us; and it is that belief which becomes the basis of our believing in ourselves. This means that our self-worth is assured.

3. We believe that God has chosen to be with us in Jesus Christ and will never leave us or forsake us. Thus, we can feel secure in our living and dying. As Paul put it, "For to me, living is Christ and dying is gain" (Philippians 1:21).

4. We believe that God's adequacy is sufficient for our inadequacy. I never preach a sermon without first praying that God's adequacy will cover all my inadequacies. Then I trust that the indwelling Christ will take over the sermon.

5. We believe that God is a God of forgiveness. At the conclusion of a sermon I preached at the Tatnell Camp Meeting in South Georgia, a young man in his early twenties handed me a note. The note read, "This document excludes you from all blame." The document he was referring to was the Bible, and the verse he had written was the following: "There is therefore now no condemnation [blame] for those who are in Christ Jesus" (Romans 8:1). The note was signed, "God's love, a friend of Jesus."

Thank you, "friend of Jesus," for the truth and witness of your note. You have reminded me and all of us of God's love and forgiveness. Because of that love and forgiveness, we do not need to fear the haunting memories of our past mistakes and failures.

6. We believe that God is able to complete that which God has begun in us. Therefore, we do not need to worry about our "imaginary fears." Our God can handle the future as well as the past.
7. We believe that God does not want us to lead fearful lives. Throughout the Bible, God's constant word to us is "fear not." Lloyd Ogilvie, chaplain to the United States Senate, reminds us that "there are 366 'Fear Not!' verses in the Bible—one for every day of the year and an extra one for Leap Year!"[3] How appropriate!

As people of faith, we believe those things about God, but the question is, when are we going to trust what we believe? "Peace! Be Still!" Jesus says.

Finally, Fear Becomes Peace
in the Aftermath of Commitment

The disciples, filled with awe, said to one another, "Who then is this, that even the wind and the sea obey him?" (Mark 4:41). The disciples suddenly recognized in Jesus an authority and power that they didn't really know or understand. "Who then is this?" They must have understood that a more intensive discipleship was being demanded. "We must get nearer to him," they were saying, "we must find out more about him." "Learn of me," said Jesus.

In reality, there was no need for the disciples to awaken Jesus during the storm. There ought to be no panic when a person knows Christ. No storm can wreck the plans of God. It was great, Jesus' breaking the storm, but there was something else even greater: simply watching him through the storm. That's what Jesus wanted those disciples to do, and that's what Jesus wants *us* to do—to watch him! Jesus wants us to commit ourselves unreservedly to him.

Someone preached a sermon that described the psychological movement of worship. The pastor suggested that we ought to move in our worship from adoration to confession, then to thanksgiving, to affirmation, and to dedication. After the service ended, a man came to the pastor and remarked, "That may be what is expected of me, but that's not the way it is. Some days I never get past the prayer of confession."

Isn't that the problem with our fears? Some days we never get past our fears to our commitment. And those are the days our fears overpower us. So how do we live a life of commitment to God? How do we disarm our fears? Here are a few suggestions:

1. Face your fears realistically. In one of the parsonages my wife and I lived in, there was a security light just outside our bedroom window. In addition, there was a shade on the window. Early one morning, while it was still dark outside, my wife screamed, "Hal, get up, quick! There's a *snake* in the bed!" I was half asleep, and suddenly those words dawned on me—"a *snake* in the bed." I must have leaped ten feet straight up!

What had *really* happened was that my arm had dropped down on my wife's pillow, and she had seen the shadow on the window shade. We were in no real danger, but our fear was very real—and we decided to face it head on. We made *sure* there was no snake around before dozing off again!

2. Live courageously. As Paul said, "I can do all things through [Christ] who strengthens me" (Philippians 4:13). Through Christ, no matter what the situation, no matter how savage the storm, I will not run. That is settled!

3. Love intentionally. If love casts out fear, as we are told, then the more we love, the less time we'll have to fear.

4. Pray unceasingly. This is the very heart of the issue. Prayer is the way we take care of our inner world. If our inner world is centered on the thoughts, will, and presence of God, there will be no room in it for fear.

5. Trust unreservedly. We are far safer in the middle of a storm *with* God than anywhere else *without* God. We must learn this if we want to disarm our fears and know peace.

Max Lucado tells of the time he went to West, Texas, to speak at the funeral of a family friend. The friend and his wife had raised five children together. One son, Paul, told about his earliest memory of his father.

It was spring in West, Texas—tornado season. Paul was only three or four years old at the time, but he remembers vividly the day that a tornado hit their small town.

His father hustled the kids indoors and had them lie on the floor while he laid a mattress over them. But his father didn't climb under the protection. Paul remembers peeking out from under the mattress and seeing him standing by an open window, watching the funnel cloud twist and churn across the prairie.

When Paul saw his father, he knew where he wanted to be. He struggled out of his mother's arms, crawled out from under the mattress, and ran to wrap his arms around his dad's leg.

"Something told me," Paul said, "that the safest place to stand in a storm was next to my father."[4]

And something ought to tell us the same thing.

A Master Strategy for Stress

I want you to know, beloved that what has happened to me has actually helped to spread the gospel, so that it has become known throughout the whole imperial guard and to everyone else that my imprisonment is for Christ; and most of the brothers and sisters, having been made confident in the Lord by my imprisonment, dare to speak the word with greater boldness and without fear.

Some proclaim Christ from envy and rivalry, but others from goodwill. These proclaim Christ out of love, knowing that I have been put here for the defense of the gospel; the others proclaim Christ out of selfish ambition, not sincerely but intending to increase my suffering in my imprisonment. What does it matter? Just this, that Christ is proclaimed in every way, whether out of false motives or true; and in that I rejoice.

Yes, and I will continue to rejoice, for I know that through your prayers and the help of the Spirit of Jesus Christ this will turn out for my deliverance. It is my eager expectation and hope that I will not be put to shame in any way, but that by my speaking with all boldness, Christ will be exalted now as always in my body, whether by life or by death. For to me, living is Christ and dying is gain. If I am to live in the flesh, that means fruitful labor for me; and I do not know which I prefer. I am hard pressed between the two: my desire is to depart and be with Christ, for that is far better; but to remain in the flesh is more necessary for you. Since I am convinced of this, I know that I will remain and continue with all of you for your progress and joy in faith, so that I may share abundantly in your boasting in Christ Jesus when I come to you again.

A former parishioner I hadn't heard from in twenty years telephoned me recently. There was a certain desperation in her voice. I remembered that she had been a youth in one of my previous churches. "Dr. Brady," she said, "I am under great stress. My problem is twofold: My husband drinks, and my father is ill and very dependent. In addition, my family has had a drug and alcohol problem. Both of my brothers have been in prison. My parents frequently say to me, 'You are our shining light. We keep going because of you. In you, we did something right.' " Then my friend tearfully paused a moment, and said, "Dr. Brady, I'm afraid that I will let them down."

Perfection is a tremendous burden for a thirty-three-year-old wife and daughter to try to carry. With that burden added to other family problems, no wonder she is under great stress.

So what exactly *is* stress? The Latin word for stress is *strictus,* meaning "to be drawn tight." One woman defined stress this way: "It's like spinning on the edge of a whirlpool—faster and faster, till I wonder how much longer I can keep from being sucked down." And the experience of stress isn't limited to this woman, or to my former parishioner. From time to time, stress keeps every one of us under lock and key. We all have been enchained in that dungeon.

Whether we like it or not, we are living in a fast-moving world. We are living in an age of tremendous advance, but we are also paying a heavy price for that advance, especially in terms of stress. And we hear so much about the negative, harmful ways that stress works itself out—tranquilizers, explosive tempers, hypertension, heart-attacks, nervous disorders, fatigue, frustration, crime sprees, premature death; the list is endless.

The apostle Paul was a master at the art of living. He had a way of facing life's difficulties, including stress, with clear insight, great confidence, and calmness of spirit. Through the Scripture, we can discover Paul's secret for dealing with stress.

Paul was in a very stressful situation, to say the least. He was writing his letter to the Philippians from a prison in Rome. Some scholars suggest that Paul's imprisonment consisted of being handcuffed by a short chain to a Roman soldier twenty-four hours a day. Paul likely assumed that this captivity had brought his missionary work to an end. And while there may have been the possibility that he would be released, the probability was that one day he would be executed.

How did Paul deal with or handle his stress? What was his secret? It can be found in Philippians 1:21. Paul says, "For to me, living is Christ. . . ." That's *it*! As simple as it sounds, that's it. Paul's relationship with God through Christ enabled him to experience freedom even in the midst of his chains.

Some stress or tension in life is normal and necessary. It's a sign of life itself. Without it, there is only death or burnout. For example, if we have work that excites us and makes us want to do our best, there is bound to be some stress. I have never prepared or preached a sermon without feeling some sort of stress.

A young pastor had just delivered a sermon at a church to which he hoped to be appointed. "How was your sermon?" his wife asked.

"Which one?" he responded. "The one I was *going* to give, the one I *did* give, or the one I delivered so brilliantly on the way home in the car?" His stress had obviously gotten the better of him!

And then there is *Christian* stress. The Christian who takes seriously the words of Jesus—"If any want to become my followers, let them deny themselves and take up their cross" (Matthew 16:24; Mark 8:34)—can hardly expect to escape all the tensions or stresses of life. Moving outside our comfort zones, whatever they are, always brings stress. Thus, the genuine Christian should never expect a life free of stress, but he or she *can* expect to find the peace of God in the midst of that stress. That is God's promise to all of us, and it is what carried Paul through his times of trial. And through this expectation of God's peace, Paul was able to use a number of ways to handle his stress.

Paul Had a Reason for Living

In Philippians 1:21, Paul says, "For to me, living is Christ. . . ." What is life to me? For Paul, it is Christ. Paul loves Christ more than anything and has made a commitment to him. For Paul, Christ is his life's priority. And because this is true, Paul believes that whatever happens to himself will be for the best. If he dies, he will simply be ushered into the nearer presence of Christ. On the other hand, if he lives and faces stressful situations, then he will continue to witness and work for Christ, for that will be the greater need.

To be in Christ is to live continuously in the atmosphere and attitude of Christ. It is to live in such a way that we are never unmindful of Christ. Leonard Griffith, the noted Canadian pastor, gives a helpful illustration of this:

> One of my classmates, an intelligent and gifted lad, contracted an illness that forced him to leave school and threatened to cut short his life. Doctors could offer no cure, and his parents broke their hearts on the edge of despair. Then a wise physician held out one hope. He said, "If your son could move to a more favourable climate he might have sufficient health to enjoy a normal life." So they sent the young man to Arizona where he picked up strength, finished his education, qualified for a profession, and lived usefully and happily for many years. He had found a climate in which he could live.[1]

That was how Paul understood Christ. To him, Christ was not just a historical figure who lived a few years on earth and died. Rather, for Paul, Christ was a living presence whose spirit fills the world. Christ was an atmosphere or climate in which Paul could live peacefully, purposefully, and powerfully, regardless of the circumstances. Paul felt that he could never be separated from Christ's presence.

In these stressful times, it is crucial to have a reason for living—a *good* reason. And a good reason is one that will be important 500 years from now, 5 million years from now, 500 million years from now. Paul's reason is Christ.

Paul Had a Different Mindset

His perspective was that of eternity, not time. So often we get ourselves in a tizzy. We say, "I've got to do this and that and be here and there, and all at the same time!" And then we pray, "Lord, deliver me from an interruption. I'm on an unbelievably tight schedule." And we wonder why we are so stressed!

Did you hear the story of the businessman who was hurrying through a rural part of New Hampshire? He stopped at a service station to ask for directions. The attendant was a bit slow in getting up, so the man yelled at him, "Hurry up, I've got a schedule to keep."

The attendant said, "No, sir, your schedule's got *you.*"

How many of our schedules have *us*? In our various and varied stressful situations, this is a good question, and it will often demand a repentant response. Time and our schedules will master us if we allow them to.

Dr. Ronald R. Meredith, a former Methodist pastor in Kansas, told of passing an old cowboy.

> "Howdy, preacher," he drawled. "Glad to see you, I am."
>
> "Howdy, Frank," I answered, "just passing by and only taking time to say 'hello,' and I must run on to town." . . .
>
> "What's your hurry, son?" he asked. I started to answer, but his question was bigger than the words he used to frame it. What's my hurry? I stood there completely chastized! "To hurry big for little reasons," he said, "is the best way I know never to live at all."[2]

But Paul's mindset was different. His perspective was that of eternity. He wasn't hurried or harried with the peripheral issues of life. Paul always began with Christ and ended with Christ. "For to me, living is Christ," he said.

The only way to handle time is to see it in the perspective of eternity and to break it down into manageable parts. We may not be able to handle all the issues of tomorrow, but we *can* handle the issues of today.

Paul Carried Very Little Interior Baggage

Frequently, we modern folk get so involved in dealing with the outward, *exterior* causes of stress that we forget all about the more important *interior* causes. It's so easy to blame our stress on the boss, the job, the neighbor, the "other people," the politicians, the situation.

And all this time, we ignore the real problem that is within our own hearts and minds.

So much of today's stress is caused by interior "monsters"—things like guilt, greed, envy, hatred, bitterness, jealousy, and resentment. As a young preacher, I remember trying to minister to a woman who had lost two children to disease and a husband to an accident. She became so stressed out that she refused to see anybody except me, pulled down all the shades in her house, and sat alone in the dark, all day long, every day. When I did get to see her, she was like a broken record, expressing her bitterness over and over again.

One Saturday afternoon several summers ago, my wife and I sat waiting in the sheriff's office in Hill County, Texas. It was the day our son had been taken hostage and later rescued by police when they were forced to take the life of the assailant (mentioned in Chapter 8). As we were waiting to take our son home, the sheriff leaned over the counter and said to me, "Encourage your son to talk about the incident and his feelings about it. He'll need to continue doing this as he deals with the trauma of the situation."

In dealing with stress, it is imperative that we carry as little interior baggage as possible. And there is a place where we can leave this baggage. In the words of Paul, "There is therefore now no condemnation for those who are in Christ Jesus" (Romans 8:1). "If anyone is in Christ, there is a new creation: everything old has passed away; see, everything has become new" (2 Corinthians 5:17). "My God will fully satisfy every need of yours according to his riches in glory in Christ Jesus" (Philippians 4:19).

Paul Had a Sense of Self-discipline

So much stress is caused by a lack of order in one's life. Tumultuous living may have its moments, but generally it leads to frustration and stress.

My friend and colleague Thomas A. Whiting described his and his wife's attending a football game at Sanford Stadium in Athens, Georgia.

The University of Georgia was playing Pittsburgh in the season's opener. Our seats were high on the second deck. We were too far removed from the players' bench to observe the actions of Georgia Coach Vince Dooley. This didn't affect us very much, however, because three rows back of us we had a coach! From the beginning of the game until the end, a young fellow shouted his admonitions to the Bulldog team. Had Coach Dooley listened to his advice, I am sure that he might have won the game! When the Georgia team took the football on offense, there was one admonition which this fellow repeated again and again: "All right, team, let's be methodical!" Unfortunately, the team did not hear him, and they lost the contest![3]

You know, that grandstand coach *did* have a point. We have to discipline ourselves—we have to be methodical—if we hope to overcome stress. As Paul said, "This one thing I do: forgetting what lies behind and straining forward to what lies ahead, I press on toward the goal for the prize of the heavenly call of God in Christ Jesus" (Philippians 3:13*b*-14).

Paul Had a Good Sense of Humor

Paul's letter to the Philippians has been called the "Epistle of Joy." Over and over again, the words *joy* and *rejoice* are mentioned. Even from prison, Paul is directing our hearts to the joy that can never be taken from us. Considering all of his writing about joy, I'm sure that Paul had a good sense of humor. I was involved in a morning prayer group where one of the ways we dismissed was to name a favorite figure in the Old Testament and tell your reasons for choosing this person. Everyone else had spoken, and it was now my turn. I said, "My favorite Old Testament character who has not been mentioned is Gideon. He trusted God, stepped out in courage, and did everything he could for God." At this point, a woman in the group chuckled and added, "And he left all those Bibles in the hotels!"

"Marty" Walker, the wife of a Methodist minister, won the twelfth Teacher of the Year Award for the Dallas Independent School District. She credited her success as a teacher to her good sense of humor. And I'm sure that her sense of humor has gone a long way toward enabling her to handle the stress and strain of being a modern-day schoolteacher.

Laughter is one of the best ways for managing stress—both as individuals and as a society.

Paul Was Diligent in His Quiet Time

We make a serious mistake when we think we can handle our stress apart from God. Without God, we are like a lamp not plugged into the source of its power. Even Jesus took time to draw aside and enter into meditation and prayer. See? Even the Lord thought that having a quiet time was a necessity. Jesus knew that God was the Source of peace, perspective, and power. And Jesus also knew that he needed to spend regular time with God.

A mountain climber made it his life's ambition to scale the Matterhorn, a peak high in the Alps on the Italian-Swiss border. When he had saved enough funds, he journeyed to the great mountain, hired the best mountain guide available, and set off for the summit. The guide literally pushed and pulled him to the top of the mountain. The winds were fierce, but the sight was breathtaking. As the mountain climber started to rise from his knees to his full stature to enjoy the beauty of the mountaintop, the wise old guide yanked him back and screamed in his ear above the fury and force of the wind, "Stay upon your knees, man, or the winds will blow you off the top of the mountain!" Grab your Bible and your devotional book and stay on your knees, or the stresses of life will blow you off the mountaintop.

This is the master strategy for stress. Paul says, "To me, living is Christ." And the same will be true for you.

Chapter 10   Anger

Fighting the Good Fight

*Again [Jesus] entered the synagogue, and a man was there who had
a withered hand. They watched him to see whether he would cure
him on the sabbath, so that they might accuse him. And he said to
the man who had the withered hand, "Come forward." Then he said
to them, "Is it lawful to do good or to do harm on the sabbath, to save
life or to kill?" But they were silent. He looked around at them with
anger; he was grieved at their hardness of heart and said to the man,
"Stretch out your hand." He stretched it out, and his hand was
restored. The Pharisees went out and immediately conspired with
the Herodians against him, how to destroy him.*

Mark 3:1-6

On the Sunday following the Oklahoma City bombing, I
preached a sermon entitled "In a Hell of a World Like This." As part
of the introduction to that sermon, I expressed my own personal
anger concerning those responsible for that terrible tragedy. And I
am sure I was not alone in feeling that anger.

I had this to say:

How could anybody do something like this? There is no cause big
enough to justify such a terrible atrocity. It just shows how sinful and
depraved this world really is. Humankind's inhumanity to humankind
is simply unbelievable. No question about it, those responsible must
be brought to justice—swift justice.

Anger was not the only emotion I felt and shared that Sunday, but it was a strong emotion. Anger and its expression can be tricky business. However, the idea that anger is a sinful emotion is inaccurate. The truth is, there is no sinful emotion. But there are sinful *uses* of emotion, and large numbers of us are in agony under the weight of those massive chains. On the other hand, anger is also a powerful energy given to us by God and can have very positive significance. Whether anger is destructive or constructive depends on how we use it.

In Mark 3:1-6, what angered Jesus was the Pharisees' distorted way of looking at things. These Pharisees put their own self-interest above humanity's needs and welfare. Right before their eyes was a person in need—a person with a withered hand. But that seemed to make no difference to them; instead, they were more concerned with preserving tradition. Faced with that, Jesus became angry.

On another occasion, Jesus went into the Temple, which was to be a house of prayer for all nations. But inside the Temple, prayer was drowned out by the pandemonium and clamor of buyers and sellers and animals. People were arguing, cheating one another and being cheated. Animals were noisy and smelly. The sounds of the "fast buck" were everywhere. Far from being a house of prayer, this Temple was now nothing but a marketplace (Mark 11:15-17).

As Jesus witnessed the domination of these false values in the Temple, he became terribly angry. And not just a passive anger; he went into action. At this point, Jesus did the most shocking thing of his entire ministry. He seized a whip and began turning tables over. He swiftly and forcibly drove the buyers and sellers and their animals out of the Temple. Jesus blazed in anger because needy people were being robbed of their chance to meet God.

Jesus also became angry when his misguided friends got in the way of little children who were being brought to him to be blessed. "When Jesus saw this," the writer of Mark declares, "he was indignant and said to them, 'Let the little children come to me; do not stop them; for it is to such as these that the kingdom of God belongs' " (Mark 10:14).

There is nothing that angers Jesus more than depriving him of the privilege of blessing and attending the little children. So great was his love for these children that he said it would be better for one to have a large stone tied around his or her neck and be drowned in the sea than to cause a child to go wrong (Mark 9:42).

What are we to make of these outbursts from an angry Christ? Did the fact that Jesus became angry make him any less divine than he was when he died on the cross? Maybe we are confused as to the real character of his divine nature. If these expressions of an angry Christ do in fact reflect the character of God, then we will have to look at anger in a different light.

Paul wrote to the Ephesians, "Be angry but do not sin" (4:26). Another way of saying this is, "Be angry, but be *constructive*."

Anger Is Constructive When We Recognize It as a Normal Part of Life

A little boy who had been punished for an angry outburst said his prayers, "Dear God, please take away my temper . . . and while you are at it, take away my mother's temper too!" But if we lose our temper, we will be less than God intended us to be. God created us with the capacity to get angry. Evidently, God recognized that our tempers have value. Author James W. Angell relates details of one woman's research into anger and children.

> In a delightful essay, Judith Viorst excerpted several interviews she had with children on the subject, "What's a good mother like?" At one point she says: "None of the children expected a mother never to get angry. 'She has to,' said Ted, 'or she'll faint from holding it in.' 'But it's best to remember,' said Randy, 'that when she starts to act real weird, you have to look scared and serious. Don't giggle. When mommies are mad, they get madder when you giggle.' "[1]

Note that the researcher said, "None of the children expected a mother never to get angry." Even the children recognized that a mother's anger is a normal part of life. That should be a great comfort to all parents in their periodic frustrations.

When I was working on my Doctor of Ministry degree, I had to take a Clinical Pastoral Education (C.P.E.) quarter. Part of the purpose of that quarter was to help the student get in touch with his or her feelings, one of which is anger. One course requirement was to present a verbatim to a couple of supervisors and other C.P.E. students. A verbatim was supposed to be a conversation you had with one of the patients in the hospital. The supervisors would ask you why you chose a particular patient, what in your makeup caused you to choose this patient, why you said what you did, why you are the way you are, and so forth. Needless to say, these sessions could get rather stormy at times, as the supervisors asked these probing questions and the student worked at giving adequate responses. To make matters worse, when you presented a verbatim, you had to sit in the middle of the group. Nobody would smile or say anything. Everyone just stared at you while the supervisors grilled away. So you can understand why I dreaded my turn to present a verbatim.

The day finally came, and I was filled with apprehension. I had prepared for my verbatim as best I could, had made a number of extra photocopies of my presentation so that everyone would have one, and felt I was as ready to go as I'd ever be. But there was a problem: One of the supervisors had called and said he was running late and wouldn't be able to be there for part of the session. Consequently, the other supervisors had to make a decision as to whether I would make my presentation that day or wait another week. After keeping me in suspense, the supervisors decided that I had to wait. This meant that I had to prepare an additional verbatim and live in dread for another week.

Momentarily, we dismissed to our small groups. When the tardy supervisor finally showed up, he asked, "How's it going?"

I replied, "Fine, all ten copies." That was *not* the thing to have said.

The supervisor said to me, "What's *that* about?"

I replied, "I'm just a little disappointed at not being able to present my verbatim today."

He said, "Disappointed?"

I replied, "Well, just a little upset."

He said, "Upset?"

I replied, "Well, just a little discouraged."

He said, "Are you trying to please me?"

Freed by Grace

At that point, I looked him dead in the eye and said, "You would be the *last* person I would ever try to please."

Immediately my supervisor and I both realized that I had gotten in touch with my anger. And that was important, because it helped me realize that anger is a normal part of life. Yes, even for a clergyperson, anger is a normal part of life.

Dr. Paul Tournier, the Swiss physician-counselor, said, "The greatest obstacle to acceptance is anger that has been repressed because one has not dared to give expression to it."[2] Tournier was saying that if our anger is to be constructive, we have to own it.

Anger Is Constructive When It Is Controlled

When I was a child, I had a ten-year-old Pinto horse named Dixie. We were very fond of each other, and I was very used to riding her. But on one occasion when we were riding through the back yard, the horse suddenly became spooked and started galloping full-speed toward the edge of the pasture. I lost control of Dixie and couldn't stop her; she ran both of us right through the barbed-wire fence. (Fortunately, I escaped with only a cut on my lip.) Dixie and I had been doing fine until I lost control. And at *that* point, I experienced disaster.

Much of our anger is weakness, not strength, because it is out of control. Frequently our anger is a response of emotional immaturity or arrested development.

I remember as a boy once playing golf with a younger friend who at the time was one of the best junior golfers in the country. We were playing in a foursome with our fathers. My young friend had hit just about every shot perfectly and was shooting an unbelievably good score. Then he missed his drive on the fifteenth tee. Immediately, he slammed his club down, lay down on the ground, and started kicking and screaming. At that precise moment, my father leaned over to me to point out that it would be unwise for me to ever behave in that manner; and I got the message, loud and clear! But while most of us have come to understand that anger in a child or baby is a normal response, anger in an adult can be quite different. The "terrible-tempered," immature adult is just not a very impressive figure.

There was a man whose car was repossessed. In his uncontrolled anger, he walked into a company office and unloaded an automatic weapon on company employees. A number of those employees were killed before that angry man finally took his own life. Nearly two million crimes are committed in the United States each year because of anger. And anger leads to a half million divorces each year.

Each year in the United States thousands of children are classified in the "battered child" category because a parent's anger got out of control. And there are growing numbers of battered wives and battered husbands.

United Methodist pastor Harry Peelor wrote of once hearing a speaker who asked his audience "to remember one thing from his address. It was this statement: 'Anger is steam.' " Peelor went on to say that "if steam is to have constructive value, it must be under control. Steam can be used to blow a whistle to make a lot of noise, or it can move things. . . . Controlled and put to work, anger is a powerful force that can count for good."[3] This is the difference between expression of anger as a child and as an adult.

As the apostle Paul put it in his letter to the Corinthians, "When I became an adult, I put an end to childish ways" (1 Corinthians 13:11*b*). As adults, we have the capacity to learn to control our anger.

Anger Is Constructive When Its Motivation Is Unselfish

Jesus never got angry over wrong done to himself; his anger was always over wrong done to others. In the Scripture, Jesus became angry at the Pharisees not because of their hatred toward him, but because of their hard-heartedness toward their neighbor in need. Jesus himself was free of hatred, malice, and resentment.

So often our anger is the result of what we feel is a personal slight: someone is late; someone lies to us or about us; someone passes us or cuts in front of us on the expressway; someone disagrees with our way of thinking; our child doesn't come home on time; our spouse forgets something important; someone ignores us.

Talk-show host Larry King said that the worst guest he ever had on his nationally syndicated talk show was the late actor Robert Mitchum. King said he just couldn't get Mitchum to engage in conversation. He said he tried everything, asked him every question, but Mitchum just wouldn't carry on a conversation. Then King said he had learned a lesson: "You can be the greatest interviewer or conversationalist in history, . . . but if someone is determined that they ain't gonna talk, they ain't gonna talk. Don't take it personally, just find another person to talk to."[4] Likewise, we need to remind ourselves that not everything that makes us angry was *intended* to do so. Realizing this, it just makes more sense to let some things pass.

In *If I Should Die Before I Live,* Arthur Fay Sueltz writes:

Columnist Sidney Harris tells of going with a friend to a newsstand. His friend gave the newsman a friendly greeting. But in return he got poor and discourteous service. He accepted the newspaper shoved at him, smiled and wished the newsman a nice weekend. As the two of them walked away from the newsstand Harris asked his friend, "Does he always treat you like that?"
"Always. The same every day."
"Well, are you always friendly and nice to him?"
"Yes, I am."
"But why when he treats you so badly?"
"Because I don't want him to decide how I'm going to act."[5]

The Scripture says, "When [Jesus] was abused, he did not return abuse" (1 Peter 2:23). When we get angry, we need to ask ourselves whether it's because we feel we've been wronged, or because we are looking out for someone else. The answer to that question should make a difference in the way we respond.

Anger Is Constructive When It Ignites the Conscience for Good

Anger is not always the opposite of love; sometimes it is love's most fitting expression. There are simply some things that will never be changed for the good until somebody gets angry enough.

Hospital conditions were reportedly horrible until Florence Nightingale got mad.

Civil rights were only a dream until Martin Luther King Jr. got mad.

Candy Lightner was devastated by grief at the loss of her thirteen-year-old daughter, who was killed by a drunk driver. Her grief soon turned into anger, and she organized Mothers Against Drunk Driving (MADD).

As angry Christians, our prayer should always be twofold. First, that God help us to express our anger in love. And second, that God help us to express our anger against circumstances, and not people. Read the text again: First, Jesus "looked around at them with anger" . . . and then he healed.

United Methodist pastor Ross Marrs says that when he was a youngster, his father would become impatient with his behavior, warning young Ross that he was learning bad habits from the other young people he associated with.

"Tell me your name" [Ross' father would insist].

He would reply, "Ross."

His father would say, "No, I mean your last name."

"Marrs," Ross would grudgingly reply.

"Spell it," his father would demand.

"M-A-R-R-S."

Then his father would ask, "Now, does that sound like Wilson or James or Altizer?" (These were the names of young Ross's chums.)

"No," Ross would respond.

Then came the lesson: "Then you are not [one of them], and you are expected not to act like one."[6] Ross was, in fact, a Marrs, and his father expected him to act like a Marrs.

Tell me *your* name, dear reader. You answer, "Christian." Spell it. "C-H-R-I-S-T-I-A-N." Does that sound like *pagan* or *unbeliever*?

Because we belong to Christ we are different, and our anger should always be constructive.

Life's Poorest Throw: Throwing in the Towel

James, a servant of God and of the Lord Jesus Christ,
To the twelve tribes in the Dispersion:
Greetings.
My brothers and sisters, whenever you face trials of any kind,
consider it nothing but joy, because you know that the testing of your
faith produces endurance; and let endurance have its full effect, so
that you may be mature and complete, lacking in nothing.

James 1:1-4

We all know people who begin whatever they begin with a great burst of enthusiasm, but it doesn't last. When obstacles appear or the going gets tough, these people tend to throw in the towel and quit.

In *See You at the Top,* author Zig Ziglar writes:

A few years ago, an international expedition was organized to climb the north wall of the Matterhorn, a feat never before accomplished. Reporters interviewed the members of the expedition who came from all over the world. A reporter asked one member of the troop, "Are you going to climb the north wall of the Matterhorn?" The man replied, "I'm going to give it everything I have." Another reporter asked a second member, "Are you going to climb the north wall of the Matterhorn?" The climber answered, "I'm going to do the very best I can." Still another was asked if he were going to climb the north wall. He said, "I'm going to give it a jolly good effort." Finally, a reporter asked [a fourth climber], "Are you going to climb the north wall of the

Matterhorn?" The [fourth climber] looked him dead center and said, "I will climb the north wall of the Matterhorn." Only one man did climb the north wall. It was the man who said, "I will."[1]

For the climber who succeeded, the one who was able to reach his goal, the thought of giving up never even entered his mind, never became part of his way of thinking. And when the going got tough, everybody else threw in the towel and quit.

There's a picture of a seascape. At first glance it appears to show a huge rock standing on the beach, blocking the view of the ocean. But when viewed from a distance, that same picture reveals a beautiful sunrise appearing just beyond the rock. The caption under the picture reads, "Obstacles are what you see when you take your eyes off the goal."

We all know parents who have given up on their children, and children who have given up on their parents. We know spouses who have given up on their mates. We know former college students who never made it through their senior year and graduation. We know politicians who have become deeply discouraged and left public service. And we even know church people who made sincere commitments but somehow got sidetracked from their First Love. So many people simply do not have the power to see their goals and commitments through. For them, quitting has become a major captivity.

It's at this point in particular that James speaks to us in the Scripture. He says, "Let endurance have its full effect, so that you may be mature and complete, lacking in nothing" (James 1:4). Another way of putting this is, "See that you persevere to the end." James is saying that as we continue to entrust ourselves and our circumstances to God, even our various attempts will produce perseverance. And perseverance will make us "mature and complete, lacking in nothing." What a profound statement! The facing of our trials and the testing of our faith can be profitable to us if we will entrust ourselves to God.

And thus, the alternative to throwing in the towel—the other side of the coin—is finding power to see things through. How do we avoid

Freed by Grace

"giving in to giving up"? There are some very practical things we can remember, which will help us when things get tough.

To Finish Something Is Much More Important than to Begin Something

But first, let's not overlook the importance of beginning something. Beginning is always the first step on the road to anywhere. In 1936, Jesse Owens returned from the Olympic Games as the World's Fastest Man. At a large press conference, the first question asked was, "How did you do it, Jesse? Four gold medals, you embarrassed Hitler in his own hometown, the Fastest Man in the World . . . How did you do it?"

Jesse is said to have responded, "Oh, I think it all began when I was just a kid back in junior high school, and my coach got us all together and made a speech I've never forgotten. The main thing he said was, 'You can pretty well become whatever you make up your mind to be.' As a young junior high kid, I looked up at my coach and shouted, 'Coach, I've already decided what I want to be: the fastest man in the world!' " It may have been a long road for Jesse from overachieving junior high youth to the World's Fastest Man, but he apparently didn't feel hindered by the challenge before him. And it just goes to show: *Beginning* is *important!*

Some time ago, when I went for my annual physical examination, the doctor said, "Everything looks good, but you need to watch your diet and become more aware of cholesterol. Watch those fats!"

Since then, I have started intentionally watching those fats—I cut out fried foods, chocolate, and things that are bad for me. It's like learning to eat all over again. Like a little boy, I've been wondering why all the vitamins are in spinach rather than in ice cream. But if I plan to hang around, then, like you, I have to take a first step. Beginning is important.

And we should also not underestimate the importance of "beginning again"—recovering from a bad happening. Consider this: A university basketball coach kept a record of all rebounds in 183 games, and he found that the team with the most rebounds won 92 percent of the games. Very few of us would be considered "All-American" when it comes to hitting the basket in the game of life the very first time we try. So we have to rebound and try a second, third, or even-later shot in life. We've all missed the basket at times. Every one of us. Some of us have even thrown up an "airball." But the important thing is that when we've made a bad beginning, we don't panic. The important thing is to rebound and try to make the next basket or shot. After all, to finish something is more important than to begin something.

The writer of Ecclesiastes declares, "Better is the end of a thing than its beginning" (7:8). Certainly it is better to have a thing *turn out* well than simply to *start* well. Dreams turned into realities are much better than broken dreams. Accomplishments are much better than failures. How we end up is much more important than how we begin.

Isn't that the point of Aesop's fable of the tortoise and the hare? After the hare makes fun of the tortoise for being so slow and plodding, the tortoise challenges the hare to a race. The fox serves as the referee, to show the racers the starting point and the finish line. As you remember, the hare starts off swiftly and gets so far ahead that he cockily decides to take a nap, resolving to get up and finish the race later. But while the hare is sleeping, the tortoise, at his own slow-but-steady pace, crosses the finish line and wins the race. This is one of the clearest illustrations that how we end up is much more important than how we begin.

A highly successful sales representative was asked how many calls he would make on a prospect before giving up. He said, "It depends on which one of us dies first." That same sales representative once made 130 calls on a prospect in one year before finally receiving an order.

The Bible puts a very high estimate on people who finish well. Paul said, "I have fought the good fight, I have finished the race, I have kept the faith" (2 Timothy 4:7). What Paul was saying here is that he didn't quit. From the cross, Jesus said, "I have finished" (John 17:4, KJV), and then he died. And in reality, most things finally come down to fighting the good fight, finishing the race, and keeping the faith.

Consider the man who was working with the poor and the homeless in New York City. Someone said to him, "Why don't you just run away from all this . . . give it up. What are you accomplishing?" The man replied, "I would like to run away from it all, but a strange man on the cross wants me to finish!"

Winston Churchill once gave a most distinctive commencement address. After enduring a lengthy introduction, Churchill is reported to have risen from his seat, walked to the podium, and stared at the new graduates. "Never give up!" he pronounced solemnly. Churchill then turned, walked back to his chair, and sat down. As the stunned students momentarily sat in silence, Churchill once again rose from his chair, returned to the podium, and announced, "Never give up!"

Somewhat afraid that they might respond improperly, the graduates never uttered a sound as Churchill returned to the podium again and again and yet again—five times in all—each time delivering the same message: "Never give up!"

I'm sure those graduates never forgot that speech and will "never give up!" Like James, who challenged us to persevere to the end, Churchill knew that to finish something is more important that to begin something.

To Finish Something, We Need to Break It Up into Manageable Parts

We simply do not take life in one big lump; it doesn't come to us that way. In God's wisdom, God has broken up this life of ours into pieces, and though we cannot handle life in one big lump, we *can* handle it in pieces. Thus, life happens to us one day at a time.

Former heavyweight boxing champ James J. Corbett understood this. He would frequently say, "You become the champion by fighting one more round. When things are tough, you fight one more round."

A renowned author got into the depths one time, and the harder he tried to come up, the deeper he went down. His first book had been a bestseller, and on the strength of that the publisher had contracted for a second book and had paid a substantial advance for it. The author got halfway through his work, and then he was stuck, petrified and unable to write a word. Day after day, he just sat there, filled with horrible thoughts of failure and bankruptcy. But his wife helped him up. She awakened him every morning, as usual, and set him before his typewriter. He was not to write on his book, however, but whatever came into his head, whether it made sense or not. Then, little by little, with all that load off of him, the writer got back in stride, and in a few months he was pounding out his book again.

What else did Jesus mean when he said, "Do not worry about tomorrow. . . . Today's trouble is enough for today" (Matthew 6:34)? Some say that the trouble with life is that it happens every day. But that's also the glory of it! And it's the daily nature of life that allows us to finish something we start by breaking it up into manageable parts.

To Finish Something, We Have to Be Connected to the Source of Our Motivation

At the beginning of the first chapter of James, James describes himself as "a servant of God and of the Lord Jesus Christ." In the Greek text, James is referred to as a "*slave* of God" [emphasis added]. This is perhaps the more descriptive term, since a servant can change masters, while a slave cannot. Here, James's referring to himself as a slave implies his total and unreserved commitment to God. Thus, James can persevere in his trials because he is sure of God—of God's love and God's purpose running through his life.

How did the Old Testament figure Joseph handle all his adversity and let endurance have its full effect, to the best of his ability? Joseph's jealous brothers threw him into a well and later sold him into slavery. His boss's wife tried to seduce him, but he remained honorable. Feeling rebuffed, the wife lied about Joseph, and he was thrown into prison. But when at last he was reunited with his brothers in Egypt, Joseph, who had risen to the position of secretary of state, said, "It was not you who sent me here, but God" (Genesis 45:8). *There's* the secret: Like James, Joseph knew God as the Source of his motivation.

A pastor was having a conference with his associates. As they sat around a rather long table, his associates asked him, "What do you think about the political situation in America today? the credibility gap in government? the threat of AIDS? family breakdown? What's your feeling about the economic depression that some people believe will strike America?" And on and on they went.

The pastor thought long and hard about their questions as he examined his own heart. His reply, in essence, was this:

I'm very concerned about the things you've talked about, but I'm not remotely concerned about holding them in my mind until they get on top of me. You ask me why? Well, these things are not my source. My source is God. These things are not stable and change, but God doesn't change. He's constant. God's always the same, and God is in the *now*.

In the King James Version of the Bible, Jesus is called the "author and finisher of our faith" (Hebrews 12:2). As the "author" of our faith, he is the beginner. As the "finisher," he sees it through. Jesus matches the finish with the start. And at every step along the difficult way, he gives his own grace of perseverance. It is in knowing Christ that we can not only begin something—and sometimes begin *again*—but also remain steadfast in God's purposes and mission.

Thomas A. Whiting describes an important lesson he learned early in his career. Still a single person at the time, he had just made the rather lonely trip to his first pastorate.

One light bulb hung from the ceiling in the living room, one in the bedroom, and one in the kitchen. Each functioned by a pull-switch. There on the mantle he saw a letter from his predecessor, who had gone into the Army chaplaincy. In the letter, the former pastor wrote: "This is a seven-point circuit. You will find more heartache here than perhaps you have at any other point in your life. Don't try to carry all of it alone. If you do, it will crush you. You will have to let God have some of it." I hadn't been there a week before I knew he was right.[2]

What is James's message to us? "See that you persevere to the end." Don't give up; don't throw in the towel. Keep your focus on God, and know that we don't have to bear our burdens or face our challenges alone.

How Do You Spell Success?

At Gibeon the LORD appeared to Solomon in a dream by night; and God said, "Ask what I should give you." And Solomon said, "You have shown great and steadfast love to your servant my father David, because he walked before you in faithfulness, in righteousness, and in uprightness of heart toward you; and you have kept for him this great and steadfast love, and have given him a son to sit on his throne today. And now, O LORD my God, you have made your servant king in place of my father David, although I am only a little child; I do not know how to go out or come in. And your servant is in the midst of the people whom you have chosen, a great people, so numerous they cannot be numbered or counted. Give your servant therefore an understanding mind to govern your people, able to discern between good and evil; for who can govern this your great people?"

It pleased the Lord that Solomon had asked this. God said to him, "Because you have asked this, and have not asked for yourself long life or riches, or for the life of your enemies, but have asked for yourself understanding to discern what is right, I now do according to your word. Indeed I give you a wise and discerning mind; no one like you has been before you and no one like you shall arise after you. I give you also what you have not asked, both riches and honor all your life; no other king shall compare with you. If you will walk in my ways, keeping my statutes and my commandments, as your father David walked, then I will lengthen your life."

Then Solomon awoke; it had been a dream. He came to Jerusalem where he stood before the ark of the covenant of the LORD. He

offered up burnt offerings and offerings of well-being, and provided
a feast for all his servants.

1 Kings 3:5-15

How do you spell *success*? How do *I* spell it?

A retired business executive was once asked the secret of his success. He replied that it could be summed up in these words: "and then some."

"I discovered at an early age," he said, "that most of the difference between average people and top people could be explained in three words. The top people did what was expected of them—and then some.

"They were thoughtful of others—and then some. They met their obligations and responsibilities fairly and squarely—and then some. They were good friends to their friends—and then some. They could be counted on in an emergency—and then some."[1]

Another person spells success in terms of "price tags." The four price tags mentioned were the following: "painstaking preparation, helping others to grow, high aim, long days and sleepless nights."[2]

Dennis Waitley, a national authority on high-level performance and personal development, lists in his book *Seeds of Greatness* "the ten best-kept secrets of total success." According to Waitley, they are "self-esteem, creativity, responsibility, wisdom, purpose, communication, faith, adaptability, perseverance, and perspective."[3]

It may seem odd to think of success as an imprisonment, but for a vast number of people in our culture, that's just what it is. These people tend to spell *success* in terms of power, position, popularity, pleasure, and wealth. You can see it written all across their stress-filled faces.

But how do *you* spell *success*? How do *I* spell it? Success means different things to different people. Success also means different things to us at different times in our lives. And sometimes we cannot even define what we mean by *success*. When Hamilton College celebrated its centennial, one of its most famous alumni, Alexander Woolcott, was asked to give a major address. Woolcott opened his speech this way: "I send my greetings today to all my fellow alumni of Hamilton College, scattered all over the world. Some of you are successful and some of you are failures—only God knows which are which!"[4]

The Old Testament's King Solomon provides an illustration of how we might spell both *success* and *nonsuccess*. Solomon had both power and wealth—but he was not always a success. The newly crowned young King Solomon *appeared* to be headed for success. In fact, he possessed two characteristics common to all true success.

Solomon Had Gratitude

In the beginning of his reign as king of Israel, Solomon exemplified a sense of gratitude. As a young king, Solomon understood that simply *being* a king would not necessarily make him a *successful* king. There were always good kings and bad kings. There were kings who did their job well and kings who didn't. Solomon realized that he would have to work at being a successful king.

In the early days of his reign, Solomon had a dream. In that dream, God said, "Ask what I should give you." Immediately, Solomon expressed his gratitude to God for enabling his father, King David, and for bringing him to the throne. Then Solomon asked God for the wisdom to govern God's people wisely.

This was an unusual request for a young, inexperienced king. He could have asked for the world—power and riches and health. Instead, Solomon prayed, "Give your servant therefore an understanding mind to govern your people, able to discern between good and evil; for who can govern this your great people?" (1 Kings 3:9).

Here Solomon points out an essential characteristic of any genuinely successful person—a sense of gratitude. Of all people, successful people ought to realize the debt they owe to others. Yet many "successful" people seem to forget.

In reality, there are no self-made people. Everyone who has ever accomplished anything has received help from others. Every one of us has had friends or family who strengthened us by believing in us and giving us encouragement.

When a running back makes a long run, there is almost always a key block that springs him loose. Some strong lineman clears the way.

I remember the years it took me to complete the requirements of the Doctor of Ministry degree. I also remember that I would never have received that degree without the kindly help of a good friend, Dr. Clyde Faulkner. Dr. Faulkner, who is the dean of the College of Arts and Sciences Department at Georgia State University, went out of his way to give me that extra help. He was always there for me with his expertise, patience, and encouragement.

In Solomon's prayer to God, he remembered all that God had been able to accomplish through his father, King David. He recalled his father's contribution to the welfare of the people of Israel. And Solomon was grateful that he would be building on his father's strong foundation.

Solomon could also have remembered to thank the prophet Nathan. It was Nathan who had challenged King David when he morally strayed with Bathsheba. Without Nathan, there would have been no throne for Solomon to rule.

I'm sure Solomon could have thanked many others—advisers, military commanders, loyal troops, to name a few. And the same is true of all successful people.

Ellsworth Kalas writes that several years ago, he offered the invocation for commencement exercises at a large state university. He recalled an unprogrammed event more than everything else. "At a strategic point, the president of the university invited the graduating students to applaud their parents and spouses, in appreciation for helping them reach this wonderful day."

Kalas added that the president of the university "might also have invited the students to applaud their professors and librarians, the authors of their textbooks and of journal articles, [researchers], and the citizens whose taxes had paid most of the cost of their education." And then, Kalas said, "Above all, the president could have invited the students to bow in gratitude to God, the Source of life, breath, health, and talent." [5]

Early on in his life, Solomon displayed this sense of gratitude.

Solomon Had Humility

Several years ago in the *Miss America* pageant, the five finalists were shown a large board filled with several different words. Each contestant was asked to select one word to define or explain in her own terms. Miss Arkansas chose *humility,* and this is what she said about it:

> Every person has wonderful goals set for themselves in their lives—to be witty, to be ambitious, to be educated, to have responsibilities. But we always look up to someone who has humility. We admire and strive for it. Every girl should have it. Every man and woman should have it. Humility is the key to success. Though it is very obvious to others, it is invisible to those who possess it.

As a new king, Solomon too displayed humility. In his prayers to God, he prayed, "And now, O LORD my God, you have made your servant king in place of my father David, although I am only a little child; I do not know how to go out or come in" (1 Kings 3:7). Solomon made this admission just prior to his asking God for the wisdom to govern wisely.

Most of us have what seems to be an "inborn drive" for success. Yet most of us find it harder to deal with success than with failure. So often we become unbalanced when success comes our way. We start to read our own press clippings, as they say. Thus, we will always need God's guidance so that we might carry our success gracefully.

Too often today, sports figures make the wrong kinds of headlines, getting into trouble of various sorts. But one sports figure who seems to carry his success gracefully is Cal Ripken Jr. A few years ago, Ripken broke Lou Gehrig's Major League Baseball record for consecutive games played, a record that had stood for decades. By Ripken's way of thinking, all he had done was play in 2,131 consecutive baseball games—just doing his job—and somebody was honoring him for it. But it wasn't just *somebody* honoring him—it was 46,000 baseball fans in Baltimore, with the rest of the world watching on television! After four-and-a-half innings had passed, making the game official, the fans in Baltimore gave Ripken a twenty-three-minute standing ovation in the middle of the game. Ripken just kept coming out of the dugout, tipping his cap, waving and mouthing the words "thank you, thank you," over and over again.

But even more impressive about the accomplishment than the tremendous ovation he received was Ripken's speech that followed. He never claimed immortality. He refused to compare himself with Lou Gehrig, whose record he had broken and who Ripken has described as a much superior performer. And Ripken thanked a number of special people for making his success possible. Blackie Sherrod of the *Dallas Morning News* wrote: "Such modesty, in contrast to the egos in today's parade, is a curious treasure, like ancient hieroglyphics found in a forgotten cave."[6]

The more success a person achieves, the more that person needs the presence of Christ in his or her life. It's the only way to keep perspective, handle correction, and remain teachable. We recall that it was Christ, "who, though he was in the form of God, / did not regard equality with God / as something to be exploited, but emptied himself, / taking the form of a slave" (Philippians 2:6-7).

But as important as gratitude and humility are, there are two characteristics that Solomon didn't possess. And lacking these, Solomon was ultimately not successful.

Solomon Lacked Faithfulness

Evidently Solomon forgot that God was more interested in his faithfulness than in his accomplishments. Without question, Solomon accomplished much. He reigned as king of Israel for forty years. After King David died, Solomon secured his royal power over his enemies. Solomon built the Temple; though it was slaves who provided the hard labor, it was Solomon who provided the vision and the leadership. Solomon was a man who achieved great wealth. He had great organizational skills and was a businessman. And Solomon was reported to be a man of great wisdom (though, in the final analysis, wisdom only in a restricted sense).

Yet with all his great accomplishments, Solomon was not faithful to God. God warned Solomon about his having many wives and building temples to their gods. But Solomon wouldn't listen; he followed other gods anyway. The result was that the God of Israel became angry with Solomon, and after Solomon's death, the kingdom of Israel was split apart.

Consider the following definitions of *success*. Methodist pastor Harry Peelor says that success is "the quality of living that finds peace and joy and victory in every experience."[7] Bishop Ernest Fitzgerald states that success is taking what life hands you and managing it so that win, lose, or draw, you may look back and not be ashamed.[8]

As well as I like those definitions of *success,* I like this explanation even better: "Anything in God's creation is successful when it functions within the purpose for which it was made." What, then, is the purpose of a human being? The purpose of a human being is to become a child of God and to discover and do the will of God. No matter what else a person may accomplish in this life, if he or she has not carried out his or her purpose for being here, then that person is not a success.

A mother was having a difficult time with her young teenage daughter's struggle for independence. Among other things, the girl was spending too much of her allowance on perfume, contrary to her mother's instruction. Disturbed by this situation, the girl's mother said, "Didn't I tell you not to use so much perfume? I can smell it a mile away!"

"But, Mother," the frustrated young teenager replied, "I love this perfume. It's called 'Gorgeous,' and I feel gorgeous."

Her mother replied, "I wish you would wear one called 'Obedient'!"[9]

Essentially, this was God's message to Solomon, and it is also God's message to us—be faithful, be obedient. But Solomon forgot! He was not faithful to God, and consequently he was not successful. God always gives a priority to faithfulness.

Solomon Lacked Excellence

Solomon did not live a life of excellence, and this too kept him from being a success. There is one standard of success that is always the same: "Have you done the very best you could?"

A woman told a concert pianist after a recital, "I'd give half of my life to be able to play the piano that well."

The pianist responded, "Madam, that's exactly what I gave."

If there's any word that successful people despise, it is the word *mediocrity.* They refuse to just get by with half efforts.

Malcolm Muggeridge titled his short biography of Mother Teresa *Something Beautiful for God.* That's the way all of us should carry on our work, whatever it is—particularly our work for Christ and the church. The preparation we bring to worship, the participation we provide, the song we sing, the class we teach, the sermon we preach, the office we hold, the service we render, the prayer we pray, the fellowship we share, the gift we give. All of it should be done with excellence, because it is being done for God.

The last performance classical composer Franz Joseph Haydn attended was *The Creation,* on March 27, 1808. As the music ended and the audience applauded enthusiastically, Haydn lifted his hands toward heaven and said, "Not from me—from thee, above, comes everything."

Because God had given the best to Haydn, Haydn had done his best for God.

So how do *you* spell *success?* I spell it this way—gratitude, humility, faithfulness, excellence.

Notes

Chapter 1: Grumbling

1. Robert Fulghum, *From Beginning to End: The Rituals of Our Lives* (Villard Books, 1995); p. 259.
2. Philip Yancey, *The Jesus I Never Knew* (Zondervan, 1995); p. 265.

Chapter 2: Inferiority

1. Reuel L. Howe, *Live All Your Life* (Word Books, 1974); p. 81.
2. Ernest Fitzgerald, *How to be a Successful Failure: The Sure Way to Turn Failure Into Success* (Atheneum/SMI, 1978); p. 23.
3. John B. Rogers, Jr., *In Him Is Life: How Christ Meets Our Deepest Needs* (Augsburg Fortress, 1994); p. 53.
4. Poem from William Mitchell's *The Power of Positive Students* (1986, out of print).
5. Wilson O. Weldon, *A Plain Man Faces Trouble* (The Upper Room, 1971); p. 70.
6. James D. Mallory, Jr., with Stanley Baldwin, *The Kink and I: A Psychiatrist's Guide to Untwisted Living* (Victor Books, 1973); pp. 92–93.
7. David Seamands, *Healing for Damaged Emotions* (Victor Books, 1988); p. 71.

Chapter 3: Loneliness

1. Harold Blake Walker, *To Conquer Loneliness* (Harper & Row, 1966); p. 1.
2. Sir Edward Dyer, "My Mind to Me a Kingdom Is," in *Home Book of Verse*, Burton Egbert Stevenson, ed. (Henry Holton Co., 1949); p. 2987.
3. J. Ellsworth Kalas, *If Experience Is Such a Good Teacher, Why Do I Keep Repeating the Course?* (Dimensions for Living, 1994); p. 23.

Chapter 4: Worry

1. Ernest A. Fitzgerald, *Keeping Pace: Inspirations in the Air* (Pace Communications, Inc., 1988); p. 184.
2. Bill Hybels and Mark Mittelberg, *Becoming a Contagious Christian* (Zondervan, 1994); pp. 217–18.

Chapter 5: Depression

1. Thomas A. Whiting, *Be Good to Yourself* (Abingdon Press, 1981); p. 77.
2. M. Scott Peck, M.D., *In Search of Stones: A Pilgrimage of Faith, Reason, and Discovery* (Hyperion, 1995); p. 395.
3. Paul A. Hauck, *Overcoming Depression* (Westminster Press, 1973); pp. 22–25.
4. Denise Topolnicki, "Workaholics: Are You One?" *Psychology Today,* July/August 1989; p. 25.
5. Herb Miller, *How Not to Reinvent the Wheelbarrow: Basic Biblical Christianity* (Abingdon Press, 1990); p. 66.

Chapter 6: Grief

1. Wayne E. Oates, *Your Particular Grief* (Westminster Press, 1981); p. 15.
2. Paula D'Arcy, *Where the Wind Begins* (Harold Shaw Publishers, 1984); page 52.
3. Doug Manning, *Comforting Those Who Grieve* (Harper and Row, 1985); p. 11.
4. Henri J.M. Nouwen, *In Memorium* (Ave Maria Press, 1980); p. 57.
5. Wayne E. Oates, *Your Particular Grief*; p. 19.
6. Bob Buford, *Halftime: Changing Your Game Plan from Success to Significance* (Zondervan, 1994); p. 56.
7. M. Scott Peck, M.D., *In Search of Stones*; p. 194.
8. Max Lucado, *A Gentle Thunder: Hearing God Through the Storm* (Word Publishing, 1995); p. 64.

Chapter 7: Discouragement

1. Thanks to Rodney Wilmoth for this story.
2. Evan Thomas, "An American Hero," *Newsweek,* June 19, 1995; p. 28.

Chapter 8: Fear

1. Frank L. Fowler III, "Breaking Free from Fear; Are You Living Your Life?" *Pulpit Digest,* July/August 1989; p. 58.
2. Elizabeth O'Connor, *Cry Pain, Cry Hope: Thresholds to Purpose* (Ward Book, 1987); p. 136.
3. Lloyd Ogilvie, *12 Steps to Living Without Fear* (Word Books, 1987); p. 24.
4. Max Lucado, *In the Eye of the Storm: A Day in the Life of Jesus* (Word Publishing, 1991); pp. 201–02.

Chapter 9: Stress

1. Leonard Griffith, *This is Living* (Abingdon Press, 1966); p. 45.
2. Ronald R. Meredith, *Hurryin' Big for Little Reasons* (Abindgdon Press, 1964); pp. 20–21.
3. Thomas A. Whiting, *Be Good To Yourself*, pp. 93–94.

Chapter 10: Anger

1. James W. Angell, *Learning to Manage Our Fears* (Abingdon Press, 1981); pp. 58–59.
2. Paul Tournier, *Creative Suffering* (Harper & Row, 1981); p. 82.
3. Harry N. Peelor, *What to Do When You Don't Know What to Do* (1981, out of print); pp. 90–91.
4. Larry King, with Bill Gilbert, *How to Talk to Anyone, Anytime, Anywhere: The Secrets of Good Communication* (Crown Publishers, Inc., 1994); pp. 151–53.
5. Arthur Fay Sueltz, *If I Should Die Before I Live* (Word Books, 1979); p. 49.
6. Ross W. Marrs, *Be My People: Sermons on the Ten Commandments* (Abingdon Press, 1991); p. 40.

Chapter 11: Giving Up

1. Zig Ziglar, *See You at the Top* (Pelican Publishing Co., 1977); pp. 122–23.
2. Thomas A. Whiting, *Be Good to Yourself*, p. 80.

Chapter 12: Success

1. Carl Homer, "Democracy in Action," *Guidepost* magazine, April 1960.
2. Lee S. Bickmore, president of National Biscuit Company, condensed from an address before the Illinois state Chamber of Commerce, October 2, 1994.
3. Denis Waitley, *Seeds of Greatness: The Ten Best-kept Secrets of Total Success* (Fleming H. Revell Co., 1983); pp. 9–12.
4. J. Ellsworth Kalas, *If Experience is such a Good Teacher, Why Do I Keep Repeating the Course?*, p. 88.
5. Ibid., p. 91.
6. Blackie Sherrod, "An Athlete's Modesty is to be Treasured Now," *Dallas Morning News,* September 14, 1995.
7. Harry N. Peelor, *What to Do When You Don't Know What to Do* (Abingdon Press, 1978); p. 61.
8. Ernest Fitzgerald, *How to Be a Successful Failure*; p. 9.
9. Thanks to Rodney Wilmoth for this story.